Praise for *The Power of Reconciliation*

'While some books peter out before they finish, this one keeps going to the end, and the third section offers some of the more rewarding pages in the book.'

Church Times

'In this solid guide, Welby, the Archbishop of Canterbury, offers advice on how to find common ground with adversaries. The author's stories about working for the International Centre for Reconciliation illuminate how to put the principles into action, and readers will appreciate his pragmatic advice. This helpful program belongs on shelves next to Desmond Tutu's *No Future Without Forgiveness*.'

Publishers Weekly

'There is something splendid and heroic about the Archbishop's commitment to reconciliation.'

Church of England Newspaper

'A book written for our times. Welby's exploration of the moral imagination, bolstered by his exquisite intellect and engaging storytelling, validate his thesis that disagreeing well "is the very cornerstone of Christian faith".'

The Tablet

'... Archbishop Justin's prose [is] approachable and perspicuous... An excellent tool to help us work towards [reconciliation].'

Premier Christianity

THE POWER OF
RECONCILIATION

JUSTIN WELBY

BLOOMSBURY CONTINUUM
LONDON · OXFORD · NEW YORK · NEW DELHI · SYDNEY

BLOOMSBURY CONTINUUM
Bloomsbury Publishing Plc
50 Bedford Square, London, WC1B 3DP, UK
29 Earlsfort Terrace, Dublin 2, Ireland

BLOOMSBURY, BLOOMSBURY CONTINUUM and the Diana logo are
trademarks of Bloomsbury Publishing Plc

First published in Great Britain 2022
Paperback 2023

A catalogue record for this book is available from the British Library

Library of Congress Cataloguing-in-Publication data has been applied for

ISBN: PB: 978-1-3994-0298-9; eBook: 978-1-3994-0296-5;
ePDF: 978-1-3994-0295-8

2 4 6 8 10 9 7 5 3 1

Typeset by Deanta Global Publishing Services, Chennai, India
Printed and bound in Great Britain by CPI Group (UK) Ltd, Croydon CR0 4YY

MIX
Paper | Supporting
responsible forestry
FSC® C171272
FSC
www.fsc.org

To find out more about our authors and books visit www.bloomsbury.com
and sign up for our newsletters

To my mother Jane Williams, my stepfather the late Charles Williams, and to my grandmother Iris Portal, from whom I learned curiosity, presence and imagination.

To the Norton Group and others who pray for me.

1942   LICHT

WEIHNACHTEN IM KESSEL   LEBEN LIEBE

FESTUNG STALINGRAD

Contents

Introduction

God then,
encompassing all things, is
defenseless? Omnipotence
has been tossed away, reduced
to a wisp of damp wool?

And we
frightened, bored, wanting
only to sleep till catastrophe
has raged, lashed, seethed and gone by without us,
wanting then
to awaken in quietude without remembrance
of agony,

we who in shamefaced private hope
had looked to be plucked from fire and given
a bliss we deserved for having imagined it,

is it implied that *we*
must protect this perversely weak
animal, whose muzzle's nudgings

suppose there is milk to be found in us?
Must hold to our icy hearts
a shivering God?[1]

The woman circles the baby in a shawl, enveloping them both. Both faces are barely visible. Her arms and body are the circling not of fear and despair but of love and faith. Were it not for the arms of the mother, the child would be exposed, vulnerable, condemned to die by weather and cruelty. She puts her body between him and the world.

Outside the dug-out where the picture – an ikon of Mary and Jesus – is pinned to a mud wall, the reality is of a frozen hell. It is December 1942, Stalingrad. The German advance of the previous eighteen months had taken them to the edge of the Volga. Here they were stopped and for months the fighting swayed to and fro, until the German forces were turned by Russian advances from besiegers to besieged. The conditions were appalling, the loss of life enormous, the suffering of soldiers and civilians immense, made worse by the callousness of the supreme commanders of both sides.

Yet, amid this frozen killing ground there were some places of hope. Lieutenant Kurt Reuber, pastor and physician with the encircled German army, having drawn the ikon, used it as a place for soldiers to pray and meditate, to find something of the love of family, of their mothers' care. He died in 1944, a prisoner in Russia, together with two-thirds of his companions captured in January 1943 at Stalingrad. The ikon escaped on virtually the last flight out. The original is displayed in the Kaiser Wilhelm Memorial Church, Berlin, while copies now hang in the cathedrals of Berlin, Coventry and Kazan, Volgograd, as a sign of the reconciliation between Germany and its enemies: the United Kingdom and Russia.

Around the margin are included three words, 'Licht, Leben, Liebe', light, life, love. The light shone in the

darkness and the darkness did not overcome it (John 1.5).
The butchery of the Russian front, with its tens of
millions of deaths, was seen clearly at Stalingrad. In films
and books, it is described[2] with scenes of horror that
are numbing. The ikon tells of hope, of peace, of God's
abundance in Jesus Christ and of human partnership in
the ancient dream of swords into ploughshares. It calls
for peace.

There is something very remarkable about the ikon.
It seems to create a dream of peace in a world of war.
It calls from another world, one full of suffering, but
one in which a woman and her child could conceivably
survive. Its marginal words tell of warmth from light
and love and of hope of life. It calls out for help and also
reassures because the child is the Christ-child, the baby
of Bethlehem, whose existence was menaced from his
birth until his death and who yet rose from the dead and
decisively changes the world. For me the ikon calls out,
'Have mercy, we want peace' on the one hand, and on the
other, 'Have hope, *here* is peace.'

Is this infant fragility really God's answer to the power
of war and hatred, to the darkness of sin? Surely God may
as well have lit a candle in a hurricane.

The human eye sees a mother in thin peasant clothes
cradling a baby who would die so quickly if abandoned,
perhaps in minutes: St John tells us this is the Word
through whom all things were made.

Yet in the world busy human eyes are too preoccupied
and overlook the mother, doubtless walked past each day
in every great city on earth, on every battlefield and in
every refugee camp. We who are safe avert our gaze from
such sadness and suspect a trick: St John says this is an
inextinguishable light that reveals the face of God.

That contrast remains true. I ring a bishop in Mozambique after a bitter and bloody attack from ISIS. I speak to another in South Sudan as the refugee camp in which he lives is shelled by rebel forces. I get a message from the wife of a close friend engaging in peacebuilding, Ebola resisting and COVID care in the Democratic Republic of the Congo (DRC), to say he has died from the virus.

I sit by someone weeping at the breakup of a relationship, or the estrangement of a child. I pray by the bed of a woman dying of COVID-19. A letter comes blaming the Church, blaming me, for failing to prevent the abuse of young people.

In all these places it is futile and uncaring – at that moment – to speak of reconciliation. Can there be change amid such suffering? Surely the tide of history will wash away any sandcastles of peace? Surely the darkness will win?

Yet for one very simple reason I turn back to the ikon. For this child and his obedient and self-giving mother, who endured so much more than can be imagined, *is* truly light, life, love. In him God is revealed in all his forceless glory and power. This is the God who draws worship not by compulsion but by fragility that is real and deathless.

The shivering child Jesus – he certainly shivered – and his sheltering mother are God's call to us that he speaks as an adult, 'Blessed are the peacemakers for they shall be called children of God' (Matthew 5.9). God has set the pattern and the means. The pattern is vulnerability. The means is sacrifice. This baby will live some thirty-three years and die on a cross with this mother unable to hold more than his dead, tortured body. This baby will be the cornerstone of stories of peace, the foundation of a community that is more diverse than any other on earth.

It will be a community that rejoices in the abundance of diversity and seeks, because of this child, to learn to love one another and the whole world. It will be an example of failure too often, but sometimes the light of life and hope. That community will be filled with the Spirit of this child so that, at its best, no sacrifice is too great to ensure that God's choice of abundance is poured into the world.

This fragility is reconciliation incarnate, made flesh. Reconciliation must be made flesh if it is going to be real. It must transform the lives of the weak, it must protect and it must go on trying even when it fails again and again. To give up is to accept, as though through scientific experiment, that the will to power of so many people is an undeniable absolute of being human. The will to power, the formation of identity through defining ourselves as what we are not, or by targeting another group as enemies, has become acceptable since the early twentieth century as being what makes for success, satisfaction, virtue.

With the will to power, coming from within ourselves, from pride and desire, there is no space for the ordinarily human, for the good community. Power hates weakness, and boasts that it never explains, never apologizes. It cannot abide reconciliation, which requires listening to another view, even putting oneself or one's group in the shoes of the other. Power will neither offer nor receive forgiveness. As a result, the enemy must be cancelled, perhaps physically, but certainly emotionally and if possible in public esteem.

Sometimes we see the light shine, the life flourish and the love shared. Sometimes enemies destroy each other not through violence but by becoming friends. When that is visible, so is the power and presence of the God of love, revealed in the Stalingrad Madonna.

PEACE AS THE UNIMAGINABLE STRATEGY

There is something a bit clichéd about wanting peace. One thinks of actor Sandra Bullock in *Miss Congeniality* playing an undercover FBI agent in a beauty contest where the only possible answer to the question about your greatest desire is 'world peace'. Yet any account of war makes it obvious that this is indeed what is needed. War can be at any scale, from bullying in the playground, the wars of words and sometime violence in families disintegrating, the vendettas in communities, riots, civil war and insurgency, or the great geopolitical conflicts. In all of them the side effect is destruction of the human spirit, ruination of lives, mental, physical and emotional harm on a vast scale, and a dark cloud of despair and anger, even among the 'winners', if any.

Among what are often called the Abrahamic faiths – Judaism, Christianity and Islam (those that in one way or another trace their history back to the Jewish Patriarch Abraham) – each has a sense of war as normally evil but a sometimes justifiable necessity, even a good. The accounts of Just War theory, or of what makes violence righteous, apply at many levels, including judicial execution and even revenge killing in family disputes. There are also accounts of what justifies the extreme action of going to war and accounts of what constitutes proper conduct in war.

I shall not discuss in detail Just War in this book. However, two things strike me. First, that there is no comparable need to justify peace, a Just Peace theory. Second, that so much effort has gone into defining the ethics of going to war and of conduct in war. International treaties such as the Geneva Conventions have been built on work originating in the Jewish scriptures (the Christian

Old Testament), the teachings of the Prophet Muhammad and subsequent interpretations, and the works of many great thinkers, especially St Augustine of Hippo (354–430) and St Thomas Aquinas (1225–1274). In ancient and modern times, women have been both prominent and essential to peace and as advocates for peaceful ways forward, yet on the whole they are forgotten. More will be said of that later.

There is a communal conscience, a voice within that says that war and killing and violent or destructive disagreement is not good. For it to become good requires justification. Peace, on the other hand, speaks for itself. Reconciliation enables harmonious difference in a way that enables all parties to flourish: reconciliation is the activity that leads towards peace, concord, the common good and well-being.

I have left out the greatest conflict, between human beings and the natural world. Here there is no obvious enemy apart from ourselves. No negotiations are possible except among ourselves. We are the worst enemies to ourselves. It is a newly identified sort of war; with the future, the young and those yet unborn, with each other, with the creation and with God. But, if this conflict is going to end and we are not going to destroy ourselves, we must find a way of living, a means of reconciliation that does not continually diminish what is around us. Climate change and loss of biodiversity constitute long-term mutually assured destruction: the launch button has long since been pushed, and the war is raging.

I've written this book as a practitioner in the area of reconciliation for many years. I do not attempt to hide two things in particular. First, that I write as a Christian and thus the content draws heavily on the

Christian Bible. Second, I do not hide my ignorance, the difficulties, setbacks and failures that are both the most common experience and the greatest frustration of any work involving reconciliation. Both my ignorance and the complexity of the subject mean that no one writer or book can complete the whole subject.

The frustration is one of the reasons for writing. It seems so obvious that it would be a better world in which diversity is a treasure, not a threat, and radically different views could be freely expressed without destructive behaviours. Competition among human beings is good, a gift to drive us onwards and give the desire to excel. Yet to seek not only to do better than a rival but to destroy them is foolishness, for in such a world all lose.

Frustration is true at all levels, from the squabbling families to the peoples at war, where the women and children flee in long, sorrowful procession and the young men and women die in agony, loneliness and fear. At its root is the sin of human pride, which affects all, including those seeking to reconcile. There is even much conflict among reconcilers and much competition for the glory of being peacemakers!

The book is in three parts that relate to each other but can be taken alone.

Part I is a meditation about definitions and difficulties. Here I look at what reconciliation is and why it is so rare. One of the mysteries of human existence is our lack of collaboration. Competition comes naturally to us. There are many reasons, but the way they show themselves in practice is bewildering and often counterproductive for all involved.

Within Part I, Chapter 1 argues that diversity and sin make conflict inevitable. Chapter 2 contrasts the reality of conflict with the age-old desire for peace, drawing above all on biblical themes. Chapter 3 looks at the resources and origins of ideas about reconciliation.

Part II is about juggling the processes of reconciliation. It draws heavily on the story of Coventry Cathedral in England,[3] and particularly on the implicit and explicit approach to reconciliation developed there. I do not argue for a moment that this is the only approach, or even the best one, but it is the best I know and is deeply rooted in the life and teaching of Jesus Christ.

There are six chapters in this part, each of them based around an action of reconciliation and reflecting especially on John's Gospel, deeply influenced by Professor David Ford's commentary.[4]

Part III moves on to the habits of reconciliation. It uses the pattern of a course for groups of people that was developed by the reconciliation team at Lambeth Palace and published in 2020, the *Difference Course*.[5] The course is held over six evenings, seeking to introduce the habits necessary for reconciliation within a group. Originally written for churches and Christian groups, it is now being piloted among mixed-faith and other faith groups, as well as secular ones, seeking to provide a means for people to start on the very long journey of reconciliation.

At the end of each chapter there is a section for reflection and discussion. It may well be best to do that with others, preferably with refreshments (food and hospitality make a huge difference in reconciliation).

The aim of this book is to encourage peacebuilding at all levels, recognizing the difficulties but turning the abstract idea of reconciliation into something that can be done throughout life, enabling the flourishing of robust diversity and disagreement without hatred. A society and a world that renews the idea of peace gives a basis for hope of differences being the seed of growth, and not of automatic rejection of all that we disagree with and of hostility towards those who disagree.

Safety for our future is not found by seeking it, but by engaging with those who challenge us. Identity is not made by defining ourselves against others in hatred and by seeking domination: the habits of reconciliation and peacebuilding liberate our identities, preserve our autonomy, increase our safety and show us the common good.

PART I

1

What is Reconciliation?

RECONCILIATION IS DISAGREEING WELL

We need 'world peace' at every level. Like the Stalingrad Madonna it is a fragile dream, never realized but often sought. Let me be clear that I do not mean that this book holds the solution to solving all conflicts and wars, or that I am pretentious enough to think I know the answer. Nor does peace mean the absence of difference, a state of universal and unanimous agreement.

I write about peacebuilding and reconciliation in the sense of seeking relationships at all levels of human life that are resilient enough to have disagreement without destruction, victory without triumphalism, concessions without degradation. Reconciliation is the long drawn-out process, extending sometimes over generations, which seeks to achieve that end.

Peace is not found by avoiding conflict but by disagreeing well.

Where conflicts arise, too often we seek to resolve them with shallow agreements, even if we know that we have only papered over the cracks. At the level of the family that may mean pretending an argument has not happened rather than facing it. At the level of the global struggle over climate change, it may mean finding a million reasons why nothing is possible or a thousand long-term solutions that involve others doing something at some point but nobody making dramatic changes now.

It is very noticeable that peace for most countries is an ideal for the naïve more than a strategic aim for politics. To take a 2021 geopolitical example, the UK's *Global Britain in a Competitive Age: The Integrated Review of Security, Defence, Development and Foreign Policy* (the UK Integrated Review)[1] has only 13 mentions of the word 'peace' in 114 pages and only two of them relate even in passing to thinking about how peace can be built. There is no mention of reconciliation and one of mediation. To put it another way, the idea that the best form of dealing with one's enemies is to make them one's friends,[2] or at least to be reconciled to them, does not appear at any point at all in the UK's 2021 foundational strategy about security in a competitive world.

What kind of story does that tell? It says that we accept a worldview of competitive existence that may lead to violence and our only solutions are defence, resilience and seeking to increase our power. Of course, it would be absurd to argue that all countries and their rulers are seeking peace. Security is an essential and a primary duty of government. However, it is equally absurd to ignore the role of reconciliation in building greater security. Europe is far more secure as a result of reconciliation between France and Germany than it has been for centuries. Merely preserving the capacity and willingness to fight would not have led to the same result.

The same applies at all levels of human life. There is more mediation than there used to be for families and households or communities, but the greatest effort in dispute management goes to litigation. Society is too often structured only for contained conflict, not for transforming the conflict into reconciliation. A historic example of the way in which contained conflict can become a process of reconciliation is in the electoral system, which seeks successfully to enable very robust disagreement to be contained peacefully through the normative – not invariable – assumption that the other side is wrong but not evil. Elections are essentially peaceful struggles for power, civil war by other means. Imagine for a moment how foolish and frightening it would be to settle the drive for power by ensuring that the major parties had militias and enough resilience to frighten the other into submission. Imagine it being normal and acceptable to solve domestic quarrels with violence. Yet both these examples were the case for centuries and still are in many places. In others there has been a dramatic change for the better. Reconciliation is possible when its aims are clear and the means are attainable.

Reconciliation does not imply agreement, but it will demand, at the least, respect for human dignity, patience with difference, and ambition for effective and practical non-violent solutions. Obvious though that may be, it is not what we do. When there is a global problem like climate change, the habit of cooperation is so unpractised globally that potential solutions become alternative competitive forms of power seeking. The same was true in the first year or so of the COVID-19 pandemic. Vaccine nationalism, vaccine diplomacy, accusations and defences – all carried on as if proving that one's own country or group of countries was right and that being right – at least in one's own eyes – would keep the virus away.

All this competition. which is carried on through the veiled or implicit threat of violence or non-cooperative competition at every level of life, seems to come from deep within us. It is part of culture and art, of religious discussion and narrative, and of psychology, anthropology and philosophy. There seems to be a sense that talk of peace and reconciliation is for the naïve, to be laughed at in satirical comedies about beauty contests, for pacifists and for futility. We prefer sanctions to peaceful solutions. Reconciliation seems not to be real enough to be made part of policy, not promising enough to seek to embed in life, not secure enough to build a healthy society. It does not merit a whole paragraph, let alone a chapter or entire section, when considering the future integrated security of a nation like the UK. Even in the household in many places the answer to domestic dispute is submit or leave.

Clausewitz wrote that 'war is the continuation of politics by other means'.[3] One might answer nowadays that reconciliation is the best answer of human beings to every form of war. War is the failure of politics. Reconciliation is the maturity of politics.

That is the heart of the dilemma over reconciliation. It is treated as unattainable, not least because it is so misunderstood. Like many virtues, reconciliation and peace are idealized in imagination, politically unexamined in applied theory and ignored in practice. Reconciliation is treated as a serious solution to destructive conflict when all else has failed and victory is impossible for all involved.

It need not be so. There are remarkable examples at all levels of reconciliation from the geopolitical to the intimate within the household. Most people will know of some among friends and family. At the international level the global violence of the years between 1914 and 1945 led to two attempts to set up a global architecture of peacebuilding. The League of Nations failed, the United Nations progresses with many failures but is still the best forum we have in the world. It has given rise to other groups, such as the African Union, which exist to call for peace and contribute to peace's resilient establishment.

Throughout human history, in most cultures there have been dreams of peace and harmony, but lives have been lived in the muddle, competition and conflict of the world. Unreconciled or seemingly irreconcilable conflict is a daily reality for human beings at every level of their lives, whether in experience or through the news.

WHY DO WE NEED RECONCILIATION?

Identity, politics, relationships between human beings at every level tend to be self-referential. In Christian thinking God's love given to us and known by the gift of God's Spirit liberates us from self-reference by turning us out from ourselves to those who are different and loving them unconditionally.[4] The nature of God's love is seen in the understanding of God as Trinity, three persons in one God, perfect in love. Love not only accepts otherness, it generates otherness[5] through seeing the beauty of the other and through the absence of tying the admiration of that beauty to one's own advantage. In his chapter on Augustine's Christology, Rowan Williams reminds us that Augustine's book *City of God* 'as a whole is a meditation on how desire is judged and reconstructed so as to release us from rivalry and violence'.[6]

Conflict is normal because unreconstructed desire and self-reference are normal in human beings. Reconciliation thus begins with the personal, seeking transformation. The different circumstances of dispute start at the deeply personal, the battle with oneself. So many people carry a sense that life is a constant struggle to be something other than they are. We even have an expression for someone who stands out on account of their inner peace and contentment, saying, 'they are happy in their own skin'. Unreconciled conflict with oneself is among the most destructive, because you cannot escape your enemy except by harming yourself, and many do, directly or through substance abuse or lifestyle. The search for contentment, for inner peace, is a staple of philosophy, drama, art and of religious life.

In the Christian scriptures it is at the heart of the ponderings of the compiler of the first book of the Bible, Genesis, in its early chapters. The story of the fall is not only Paradise Lost, as in Milton's great poem, but also the loss of human harmony and peace, within Adam and Eve as well as between them. Their desire brings wrong action, not enjoying the otherness of God and relishing God's love, but grasping at what they do not have. On being discovered in their guilt they are ashamed, a deep-felt inner reaction. As shame so often does, it leads them to blame each other and then Satan. The loss of peace leads to the first human division.

Very quickly, conflict expands from words to deeds, as their children, Cain and Abel, argue and Cain murders his brother. Death by violence spreads through the generations and contaminates the whole human race. The spread is impelled by desire and self-reference, not by love. Desire is imitated, and develops in its perversion of love.

In these passages, which go on and expand evil into a world where virtue is the exception, there is a sense of the writer raising the problem of conflict. Where does it come from and how can it be resolved? It is no mystery that animals fight, for they lack the ability to reason and project forwards in time beyond themselves. When our dog sees a chocolate biscuit on the floor, she cannot work out that it is there by accident, that chocolate is bad for her and will make her ill. It's food now, and no more thinking is required. If another dog is also going for the biscuit, the only question is which is stronger (actually our dog is a wimp so she would leave the biscuit if in competition with a lethargic mouse, but that ruins the illustration).

Human beings are different. We can reason. We can see the consequences of actions we take. We can work out probabilities of something giving us pleasure now but an ocean of suffering later. To some extent that is often an attraction in doing wrong; the excitement of seeking escape from consequences is part of the temporary delight of sin. At a societal level we are under no illusions as to the cost of conflict, whether with those around us at work or at home, or in the community, at a national or global level. Yet we go ahead, with reasons so weak that we all know that they cannot carry the weight needed to excuse us.

At the grandest level we come full circle and find ourselves confronted with ourselves again, this time collectively. Nuclear conflict involves mutually assured destruction, yet at least nine nations in the world have armed themselves with nuclear weapons knowing that to use them is collective suicide and in some cases the end of the human race. Climate change is the other global menace where our survival is at stake. Even in very bad scenarios of unchecked rises in temperature, most human beings would survive, but huge numbers would die and large parts of the earth become to some degree uninhabitable. The quality of life for survivors would be greatly reduced. There would be wars as the desperate migrated and wars over remaining resources. Yet there is a perceived first-mover disadvantage (the opposite of nuclear warfare where the first mover might gain a notional and temporary advantage and can convince themselves falsely and fatally it is more) that leads to inertia on a global scale. All rationality is gone.

This picture of conflict is horseshoe shaped. At one wing is the unreconstructed desire within each of us. It widens until, at its broadest, it is some of us against others of us. It ends with all of us against all of us. Both climate change and nuclear warfare are circular firing squads, the proverbial climax of stupidity in conflict.

We all know this, yet whether one is an optimist or pessimist about human nature, most people assume that conflict is just part of the package of life. We feel, if we think about it at all, that human beings have been in violent conflict as long as there have been human beings. That's the way of the world.

Wars of survival are explicable. Changes in climate have always been drivers of migration and thus conflict. Conflict provoked by a justified fear for survival requires enormous virtue to avoid or resolve since it calls for collective sacrifice. We have very little experience of such challenges in the most prosperous parts of the world. As a result, the COVID-19 pandemic exposed a deep desire to preserve ourselves even though most people accepted that the pandemic cannot be halted anywhere until it has been halted everywhere. Rationally, global cooperation is indispensable to individual security. Practically, there is a temptation of 'everyone for themselves' or, as the French saying goes, *'sauve qui peut'* – let the one who can, save themselves.

In smaller groups conflict also occurs naturally. There are obvious parallels between the squabbling seen in groups of apes to those seen in a household. Much of it will be about identity and independence. There are levels of natural competition that in a functional household lead to bickering and irritation but do not go beyond that. The rows are sorted out, affection deepens, respect for difference increases and love prevails. Similarly, in small communities like offices and other workplaces, petty irritations lead to sharp remarks. Usually these are around using the last of the milk in the common fridge or leaving the photocopier without paper.

So far, so natural and so unremarkable. The desire for survival and for adequate resources of shelter, food and water drive some competing groups into violence. Communities bicker. But, beyond the obvious are deep mysteries about the reasons for the self-destructive nature of human violence in conflict, even at the very local level. Most of us have either experienced or know of destructive conflict in the family or household. The same is seen in business partnerships, in voluntary groups, in political parties, in churches and in small communities where it is obvious to all that both the values of the group and the interests of success will be lost by further conflict. Yet many seem to prefer to rule over the ruins of their cause or group than to serve humbly and see it triumph. In Christian thinking the response of God to the sins of pride and self-reference that drive conflict is seen in the great Christian symbols of the cross and the empty tomb. The language of love '*begins* with the primordial "non-worldly" love enacted in Christ'.[7]

The mystery of mutually destructive conflict is at its deepest in our own times, although, as we have begun to see, it occupies the writers of the Bible back to the earliest parts of Genesis and to the last parts of the Book of Revelation. Why destroy what is valued, why engage in destructive conflict when the outcome is lose-lose?

WHAT THINGS PROVOKE CONFLICT?

The question of identity, who I am and who we are (which includes what 'we' means), is core to any understanding of conflict. The search for identity and the means by which it is established are dominant questions around the world. With the advent of social media identity clashes have become some of the main components of social discord. The result is a terrible confusion of quarrels in which complexity gives way to oversimplified binary definitions.

Identity may be given
We accept the identity that someone or something has given us. Historically, that might be slave or free. In the nineteenth century before the American Civil War people of colour in the slave states were assumed to be chattel slaves, which Whites could not be.[8] If you were the child of a slave, you were the property of the slave's master and even those such as Jefferson saw the breeding of slaves as more profitable than the economic use of them. Being a chattel slave was an identity bestowed by birth. There was no choice.

In the middle belt of Nigeria, in many places people are categorized either as an indigene or a settler. The settlers were often ethnically Hausa, Muslims imported by the British in the 1930s from northern Nigeria to work the copper mines. Ninety years later their identity is still 'settler', with consequential impacts on where they live and on university places. In India, caste – or being outcaste or of tribal origin – is still a formative although not always finally definitive influence on a person's future.

Conscription in the UK in the Second World War drew millions into battle because they had inherited being British. Unless they were very determined conscientious objectors, they would find themselves serving in one way or another.

On a far lighter note, in Liverpool when I worked there at the Anglican cathedral the first question I was asked was 'Are you Red or Blue?' (supporter of Liverpool or Everton football clubs). When one asked the question back, the answer would be 'X, my family has always been X.'

At their worst, imposed identities are inescapable and compel a person to be on a side in a conflict that they may neither want, nor have the power to change. Under the Nazi regime of 1933–45 in Germany a person was non-Aryan if they were one-quarter Jewish and, if so, would find themselves marked as such on identity papers. At one-half they were considered Jewish. Their religious faith, war service, skills and attitudes to being Jewish had no impact. They were targeted for extermination.

In societies where there is a culture of vendettas, the imposed identity may compel both taking sides and hatred of the other. The Nuer and Dinka peoples of South Sudan have in the past operated a vendetta culture that could oblige revenge against another clan within the tribe for more than one generation.

Finally, one may inherit or be born with other characteristics that in the eyes of the outside world determine the answer to identity even today. They may be around sexuality, education, family name, height, even hair colour. Articles about the prime minister of the UK, Boris Johnson, almost always define his character by reference to him going to Eton, implying that his schooling is his identity.

From the breadth of the examples, it can be seen that an inherited or imposed identity has throughout human history probably been the most common way of answering the question 'Who am I?' To be born in a certain place of certain parents at a certain time determined much of one's life experience, not through events that one could choose but through a history one inherited.

We may attempt to choose our identity

That sense of being done to rather than doing – our identity being defined by others – challenges the modern and western sense of having a right of choice as to who we are and what we are like. If the first way is imposed and usually communal, the second is deliberate and often individual or part of a small group resisting larger conformist forces. A phrase often heard is 'I don't want to be defined by …' The defining aspect can be birth or part of how one experiences life or expectations coming from experiences of sexual orientation, race, gender, disability and more other matters than can be described. This second way in which one can find an objective identity is often portrayed as being by choice or by declaration about oneself. There is claimed to be an element of conscious action.

However, one's actions and choices are often no more effective at avoiding conflict with oneself or with others than the act of submitting to the choices of others and being swept along in the stream of historic or cultural identity. The formation of a chosen identity is very frequently on a negative basis. I choose to be x and define x as not y. It may be linked to being in control or regaining control of life. While inherited identity or birthed identity is often a root of the most profound injustice, chosen identity is sometimes experienced as no more adequate in facing the great issues of life.

In 2016 the London *Daily Telegraph* published a long article revealing that the person I had thought was my father was not and that my genetic father was someone else. There was much discussion about the consequences and anxious questions from friends and colleagues about how I felt. My answer was that my identity was not found in DNA but in Jesus Christ. In my own experience, much identity seeking is a search for truth. I may experience myself being different from how I have been brought up. The question then arises as to how I find my true identity, or even create an identity that is closer to the truth of what I really am.

This is where a choice lies. For me, to trust God's love revealed in Jesus Christ was to put myself in the hands of perfect love that knows me perfectly, the good, the bad and the ugly. It is to be accepted by love beyond measure. Another choice is to seek to define oneself.

The group of those who refuse to be defined *by* others too easily becomes a group that defines itself as '*not-the-other*'. The definition of a group of individualists will almost always be negative if it is to enable an alternative sense of identity. The negation of accepted and imposed identities is in itself an identity, but one that is designed to lead to distance and thus to opposition.

The major difficulty with self-identification is that it ignores reality.[9] Our capacity to self-identify comes from numerous influences outside ourselves. It depends on our parents conceiving us, on their nurture or lack of it, on the way in which we are reared. It is found from them genetically. Our culture or faith sets expectations that may be very difficult to break. The radically self-referential attitude of Descartes (I think therefore I am) is behind so much of the modern attitude to my rights to autonomy. It fails, however, to note that I am also because of many others. I exist because a community exists that conceived me, formed me, cared for me, educated me, loved me. No one is autonomous, and thus no one is truly free to form their own identity except within the constraints of community, which will vary greatly in its impact.

Honour or shame may define my identity
This subject is immensely complicated and is different in each culture but common to most. It lies at the heart of many long-lasting conflicts and is a reason for the difficulties that reconciliation poses. It draws in ideas of justice and forgiveness that may become either the greatest possible barriers to reconciliation or its most solid foundations.

Honour is a word that we associate with an earlier era in many parts of the world, and shame is often treated as a sort of psychological condition.[10] Yet even when concealed by other words and concepts, they remain deeply rooted as motivations.

Within Christian understanding, honour and its companion, pride, are meant to be transformed. In St John's Gospel, chapter 13, Jesus begins the last supper he has with his disciples (a Jewish Passover meal) by washing their feet. It was the job of most guests to wash their own feet, of a slave to do so for an important guest only, and was considered an immense courtesy when offered by a householder, reserved only for very special guests. For Jesus to do this was to upturn the ideas of honour and shame and to replace them with sacrificial love-in-action. It eliminates hierarchy. In John's Gospel it prefigures in some ways the summit of Jesus' glory in his being 'lifted up' – crucified, the death of a criminal.

The early disciples in the first centuries of the Church continued to challenge honour as a measure of self-worth in contrast to Jesus' call to humility. However, both before and especially after the Constantinian toleration, which effectively legalized and approved the Church in the Roman Empire, the human desire for status and honour, embedded in classical societies whether Greek or Roman, largely replaced the costly ideas of humility.

Relational identity: the heart of reconciliation
A fourth form of identity is neither imposed nor chosen nor instinctive and cultural, but is one that forms out of relationships with others, including those with whom we disagree and those who are of little account in the public eye. It is at this point that the pessimism of this chapter begins to lift. As we rejoice in love and self-giving, we can begin to see ourselves becoming more than we inherited, more confident in our worth, and more than we could choose by ourselves. Joy and flourishing are the result.

Our identity is capable of changing and being transformed at any point, and neither birth, nor behaviour, nor culture finally fix who we are. Neither adversity nor heritage are destiny.

In Christian thinking, hope is rooted in ideas of repentance demonstrated in action by a commitment to a new way of life and to the resources of God, mediated very often in community. There are strong similarities in other faith traditions.

The monastic tradition in Christianity was, from the sixth century CE, deeply shaped by the Rule of St Benedict, who founded the monastery of Monte Cassino in Italy and is generally considered the pioneer of western monasticism. His short rule sets out a vision of communities in which the members are shaped in their identities by mutual obedience and love, by common ownership of goods, by prayer singly and together, the study of the Bible and daily work. For its time it was a deeply humane document and was so influential that it can be said to have helped rescue European civilization from the Dark Ages. Although other forms of Christian monasticism have grown up over the ages, the influence of Benedict is visible in their form of life.[11]

In 2016 at Lambeth Palace, we began an experiment in community. We opened the Palace to up to fifteen residents from all around the world, all Christians but of any church tradition, and to an equivalent or smaller group of people based in London, who would take part in the community on a part-time basis. They were men and women, between twenty-one and thirty-four years old, who came each September and stayed until the following June. This 'Community of St Anselm' was led by an Anglican dean working in cooperation with brothers and sisters from the Chemin Neuf Community, an order of Roman Catholic monastic communities of ecumenical vocation and experience founded almost fifty years ago.

It has been transformative both for its members and for Lambeth Palace as a whole. The Community has a

Benedictine contemplative aspect, with silent prayer and regular Offices (times of common prayer) in the Church of England form. It is Franciscan in a commitment to working with the poor and excluded in London. It also draws on the Spiritual Exercises of St Ignatius, a process of self-examination.

There have been ups and downs. To bring together Christians from New York and Pakistan or South Sudan is to mix cultures and ways of finding identity on a grand scale. The heart of the Community is a common purpose, to draw closer to Jesus Christ in a way that will create habits that endure a lifetime. No subject is off-limits, but the ways of interacting are guided. The result has been fruitful in love, in depth of spiritual life and in the atmosphere of Lambeth Palace as a place of prayer centred in Christ, not merely an administrative centre.[12] The Community changes our collective and individual identity for the better.

At the heart of this experiment is the desire for a life with God in Jesus Christ. Our identity is to be oneself in encounter with another, jointly serving and worshipping Christ. The Community does not create clones, but embraces and develops diversity, enabling the liberation of identity in reconciliation with others. Conflicts become points of growth.

True community, whether in one place at one time or extended widely across a geographical region, is rooted in the authority of others to summon me to responsibility regardless of hierarchy.[13] Where I acknowledge the other as being in one sense or another part of myself, I find my identity more fully in responding to the other's need.

John Sachs[14] commented that 'the saints are the selves where extreme joy and extreme responsibility converge'.

To put it bluntly, identity is not found in a passive acceptance of how I am born, nor in a passionate rebellion against the fate I have been dealt, or in conformity to self-aggrandizing ideas of honour and shame, but in extreme and joyful acceptance of mutual responsibility with those unlike me, in need of me and whom I need even though I may not be aware of it. It is in such responsibility and joy that we find *reconciliation*.

Releasing the sense of mutual responsibility and joy in relationships of difference, which is implicit within the idea of reconciliation, opens core themes of how we love and deal with diversity, and restores to reconciliation the meaning that is so often lost in a fuzzy fudge of niceness without either joy or responsibility.

The illusions of overspeed and overreach

In secular thinking, reconciliation is an event that takes place quickly and then everyone moves on. It is basically a 'kiss and make up' event, where a gesture, an agreement, a proclamation or a treaty tells everyone that 'we are now in agreement', and we all hold our breath and hope for the best.

Yet this shallow approach seldom succeeds, because it engages either in overreach or in overspeed.

Overreach is the setting of entirely unrealistic goals that are of themselves so frightening in terms of their emotional demands that conflict parties do not feel able to engage even in the beginnings of a process. The potential cost seems overwhelming. They cannot imagine what seems like the possibility of losing something that makes them who they are. At the beginning of seeking to engage with those who have done great harm, or who are perceived as such (I will return to perception and reality in Chapter 5), the pressure of the journey feels overwhelming.

Overreach is usually related to those who are supporting or assisting with reconciliation oversimplifying things. You do not resolve human problems of conflict, whether in a family or at a global level, by pretending that they are simple.

Imagine a family that is experiencing problems between husband and wife. The marriage adviser finds that the wife has committed adultery. As the conversation goes on it appears that the husband is constantly critical, neglectful and goes out with his friends all day every weekend, playing golf. Then it comes to light that a teenager in the family has mental health problems that the husband blames on the wife, which disrupt the times she has set apart to spend with the husband. Further enquiry would show that this pattern of blaming others was the one the husband grew up with and that he was never allowed as a teenager to go out with friends. And so on. Like most people the couple have many different aspects of strengths and weaknesses. The way each finds their identity and value depends on foundations for life that are complicated. Each needs a series of changes in themselves and the other if there is to be any hope of renewing the relationship.

Overreach is to say to the husband: 'Just forgive her for the adultery.' He feels dishonoured by the over-simplicity, she feels abandoned and blamed. Neither may be seeking reconciliation if that is what it means. Simplicity brings everything down to one issue. For the person involved with encouraging and supporting reconciliation, one issue is manageable. As a result they try to simplify the complexity.

Another key cause of failure is overspeed. I remember clearly a leader in Northern Ireland being interviewed on the radio in the early summer of 1998, a few weeks after the Good Friday Agreement. The first questions were as to whether reconciliation had been achieved. I cannot remember the answers, but the idea that something called reconciliation could be achieved in weeks after thirty years of the Troubles and several centuries of bitterness was absurd. Reconciliation takes time, and Part II of this book will look at the process involved, while Part III considers the habits that are required to be developed over time. A UK programme of exercise from the National Health Service is called 'Couch to 5k'. It lasts nine weeks with three 'runs' a week. The first week is very limited, a few minutes walking and running. It has been very popular. If it was called 'Three Marathons a Week from Day 1' nobody would try it.

Yet reconciliation, the emotional and relational equivalent of a marathon, is assumed to be something that gets us from broken relationships in a family, or war in a country, to 'happily ever after' in a short process. It looks unrealistic because it is.

The idea of reconciliation within the Christian tradition is the very cornerstone of Christian faith. Whether in a secular or sacred context it sets a framework for understanding the idea that it must be at the heart of the practices of any functional group.

The living world of reconciliation

Reconciliation is first a lived experience. It takes time, develops habits (see Part III) and turns into a way of life and, above all, of relating. It transforms relationships. The monastic tradition sought to live out this idea in imitation of the lives of the earliest disciples in the Acts of the Apostles. St Benedict, in his Rule (RB) sets out several times that private property is forbidden, as in the last verses of the Acts of the Apostles, chapters 2 and 4. That was only one part of the common life. The monks are to live in obedience to one another, based on length of service and mutual love, as well as to those set above them in the monastery. In so doing they are to find their true individuality through unity and mutuality.[15] Historically, the monastic life at its best set a pattern for the whole Church, both of how to live and of inspiration to do so well.

Living well meant first that Christians must live incarnationally. Jesus' birth and life are referred to as incarnational; the Christian understanding of Christ is God made flesh, living in God's world as fully human. Incarnation is part of God's process of reconciling humanity with God, of reaching across the difference and breaking down the barriers of human failure and selfishness so that human beings can live in this world in justice and equality in the presence of God. The global Church – meaning the body of Christians – is commanded by God to live incarnationally, so that looking at Christians in every culture Christ is made visible. For that to happen, Christians must be reconciled reconcilers. Reconciliation is a visible change.

Second, at the heart of Christian living is the call to sacrifice: as Jesus puts it, each of his disciples is to take up their cross and follow him (Mark 8.34). For Jesus, the way of obedience to God was the surrender of his life, a willingness to sacrifice himself through crucifixion so as to make eternal life possible for all human beings. That sacrifice was an essential part of reconciliation with God on behalf of all humans. Taking place on the first Good Friday, it was followed on the third day by the first Easter, the resurrection of Jesus to life. Resurrection is the reality of the future, of the eternal life with God offered to all human beings. In the Bible there is the promise from God of a foretaste of that life through God's life living in us, the life of purpose and love that is experienced both now partly and completely in eternity. Sacrifice is thus core to reconciliation, something to be looked at more closely in the next chapter.

A key theological idea in reconciliation is its completion. It is a journey, but one with an end in full achievement. In technical theological language, this is about eschatology, the completion of all things and the establishment of God's rule on earth and in heaven. At that point reconciliation is completed, judgement is carried out, justice is done, and all truth is seen in the light of God.

Incarnation, crucifixion, new life, completion – these words in themselves represent a long period of time. Reconciliation must be lived out and grown into. It is sacrificial. It will only be completed when perfect justice rules the earth.

There is a very human and natural use of the word and idea of reconciliation that means a sort of compromise. There is the thought that reconciliation is achieved by everyone meeting in the middle in a sort of huggy and wet mass in which nobody is really happy, and we all pretend to agree.

Nothing could be further from the truth. Reconciliation demands truth and justice, recognition and expression of anger. Forgiveness is only real when freely offered without manipulation, and freely received without compulsion. Reconciliation accepts difference because in God we see difference in perfect unity. It is costly because God won it only though sacrificing Jesus – God – on the cross. It is liberation and joy as the resurrection liberated Christ from death. It will be completed, and all will be well, all will be in the light, and all indignity, injustice and oppression will be overcome in the end. In the meantime we travel determinedly and hopefully

In earthly and human processes of reconciliation all the elements of progress towards justice have to be visible. When we consider the issues of racism, especially against people in or from the Caribbean and Africa, now in the UK and USA, reconciliation is needed. The oppression goes back to the racism of slavery, the indignities and economic control of freed slaves and their descendants through Jim Crow laws and other means. It links in to colonialism in West Africa. The sin includes the practices of racism in Europe and the USA to this day. Such reconciliation cannot be achieved through ignoring the bitter injustices and evils of past and present. It cannot be done by saying to the descendants of victims and to contemporary sufferers today, 'Well, let's just forgive and forget.' That is the position of the powerful and the privileged. It cannot be through turning all the varieties of injustice into one mass and calling it by a single word or expression. Reconciliation will require enormous care.

Reconciliation in this area demands a long period of incarnational living in which the wicked practices of misuse of power and privilege are put aside, confessed and repented. There must be repentance and reparation, the powerful undertaking sacrificial establishment of what ought to be. There must be new life in justice. There must be a vision of a truly just and equal society. In other words, the kind of world of which Jesus spoke when he taught about the kingdom of God is one that must continually be sought in the world, and lived in the Church. Until all that is done we cannot say that reconciliation between races has been begun adequately.

Reflection on John 21[16]

The last chapter of the Gospel of John functions as an epilogue but also as a pointer to the future. It explicitly sets aside any claim to be a complete biography of Jesus, but its strong and vivid three-part narrative structure tells stories of responsibility and joy, among many other things, which engage the reader at the deepest level of emotional and creative imagination.

Following the crucifixion and resurrection seven of the disciples of Jesus are in Galilee and decide to go fishing. They catch nothing all night. The work is that of normal life, with all the frustrations and struggles of wet nets, darkness, and nothing caught. By the morning they would have been tired and frustrated. Suddenly, as they are packing up, a figure on the shore tells them to throw their nets to the other side. Another frustration. Perhaps some memory of previous occasions captures their minds for a moment, and they become open to the possibility of the presence of God. They do as they are asked.

The catch is overwhelming. They realize the presence of the risen Jesus as the figure on the shore and, filled with joy, they take the huge catch to the beach, Peter diving overboard and swimming ahead. When they arrive, they find a fire, Jesus himself, and fish cooking with bread. Here is the reality of Jesus Christ. He is there among the normal, not in a special place but in daily life amid mundane tasks. The miracle of the catch is dramatic but is part of God's choice for his world. Its meaning is profound as it points to their vocations, to their future and to the abundance of the joy that Jesus brings.

But there is shame. This is the Jesus they had let down. This is the risen Jesus whom they had been meeting, but could he still trust them, walk with them, lead them? For Peter there is the warped and misshapen sense of a relationship damaged by Peter's denial. It is morning but the new day seems clouded by regret and worse. And there is ignorance. Why has all this happened? What does it mean? As in their night of fruitless fishing, they have no clear direction. Are they to go back to where they were before he called them?

But they find three things they need. There is a fire, warmth and comfort after a cold night on the lake. There is food, both that they have caught and also already prepared. Their physical needs and low mood will be met. There is the sort of love and conversation that faces any lingering sense of their own sense of failure in the past and shows them, in a sign, the way forward. They are to reach the world. Their life's purpose with Jesus is only just beginning.

These beautiful passages contain a vast richness of meaning. The only other encounters with Jesus they have all had since the resurrection have been in a locked upper room in Jerusalem where he appeared, breathed the Holy Spirit into them and commissioned them. Yet at the crucifixion the other three Gospels and John record that they had run away, and that Peter had denied Jesus three times.

Relationships as close and tumultuous as they had with Jesus during the three years of his earthly ministry have been damaged by their failures. The story of Jesus with Peter shows a level of self-doubt in even the leading disciple, despite the resurrection appearances.

Who would have been confident to meet Jesus at this time? The world is different and so is he. He has died and risen. They have failed. He comes to them where they are most at home. He gives them an abundant catch of fish, so great that it overwhelms their resources. He enables Peter to cancel out his three denials with three affirmations. They are warmed, loved, restored, all by the one who is the more powerful. He demands nothing of any but Peter, and only words from him.

Reconciliation is a gift of sacrifice. It is costly. This moment of revealing a future – for disciples, for the Church at its birth, for the world in the new age of resurrection – follows the crucifixion, the life of God given in humility and pain. Yet that pain opens the way to living in the purposes of God.

Their journey of doubt and failure has ended in a place of abundance and joy. They are at home with Jesus. It is not the entirety of reconciliation; they have their lives ahead of them, which will involve endurance and suffering. Yet the journey has begun. They have a future liberated from their past.

Summary

- Reconciliation involves the transformation of fear and exclusion of others into abundant joy in relishing difference.

- Reconciliation is the transformation of destructive forms of conflict and disagreement into the capacity to disagree well.
- Reconciliation is the experience of a journey of liberation through transformation of where and what we have been. As we see in John 21, its impact comes from at least one party demonstrating that the past need not entangle us for ever. The person or group that is more powerful must be the first to begin the journey, to set aside the power they have and to offer what is needed to the weaker.
- Reconciliation is always a process of gift and responsibility, not just for the outcome but for the flourishing of those involved. It changes the nature of relationships and gives them a way forward. So why is it so rare?

POINTS TO PONDER

- How do most of us understand the meaning of 'reconciliation'? What does it look like in films and stories outside the Bible, in everyday life? Do we have the right morally or freely to reject reconciliation with God, or with others?
- What true stories do you know of reconciliation? What are the key elements that went into reconciling?
- What do you think of as the greatest challenges that need reconciling, at any level, but certainly including yourself or your household and community and certainly including something on a grand scale?

Biblical Reflection

In this and the next two chapters a New Testament biblical passage will be offered as a basis for further reflection. For those of other faiths or those who prefer not to engage in this way please find an equivalent. These are not intended as exam questions! Before doing them, preferably with other people, be silent for a moment or pray aloud for guidance, and be honest about what you think. Don't worry about being right or wrong.

Colossians 1.15-20
This is probably a very early hymn or a statement of belief. In it Christ is described as the agent of creation and the means of reconciliation of all things to God. Creation and reconciliation are thus linked, and it is implicit that there is a conflict to reconcile.

- What does this say to you about the scope of reconciliation? Is there anything outside God's purposes of reconciliation?
- What does it say to you about human response to the possibilities of reconciliation?

2

The Hindrances to Reconciliation

If reconciliation is such a good thing, why is it so rare?

Almost half of all conflicts within countries restart in less than ten years after a ceasefire. Families seem to struggle with conflict from one generation to another. Neighbours find it easier to live miserably rather than make peace. When we get beyond the national to the global the old saying by Samuel Johnson that 'Depend upon it, sir, when a man knows he is to be hanged in a fortnight, it concentrates his mind wonderfully' is proved wrong. For example, climate change is itself a form of conflict between human beings and the planet, one which humanity is bound to lose. In addition, it is a significant driver of human conflict. It is clear beyond any doubt that climate change poses a high probability of catastrophic global impacts in every area of life. Yet far from concentrating the minds of the world, the changes that need to be made are ignored or hidden by unrealistic techno-optimism. That is not a concentrated mind; it is castles in the air.

What makes people act against their own happiness, their own hopes, their own interests so that rather than choose to search for ways to live in harmony, at least in some kind of working relationship across difference, they engage in mutual destruction?

In many parts of the world where resources are adequate or peace has been long established, this will seem to be pessimistic. Yet in other places physical war is the norm, and even in the most prosperous countries culture wars, cyber wars and campaigns of disruption proliferate without attempts at settlement.

In this chapter I want to suggest four areas that delay or destroy hopes of reconciliation. First, as we have seen, reconciliation always involves sacrifice and thus requires a willingness to give something up. Second, reconciliation challenges our explicit or implicit sense of honour and shame. Third, in reconciliation we often forget the impact of long-term trauma and conflict on the whole human being through changes in the neurochemistry, with impacts that are even transgenerational. Fourth, reconciliation is a long-term process and it is natural to look for short-term fixes to problems that will take years or even generations to resolve.

SACRIFICE

In Christian understanding the greatest reconciliation is God's action through Jesus to reconcile human beings and all creation to God. The Bible begins with the breaking of the relationship between the creator and the creation through the disobedience of the supreme point of creation, human beings. That disobedience is attributed to many things, but at their heart is the issue of pride. Human beings, in the story Adam and Eve, wanted the knowledge of good and evil. In other words, they wanted to decide for themselves and to disobey God in order to have more power.

It is a familiar story. One of the most destructive events that can happen in a marriage or equivalent relationship is unfaithfulness, cheating on your partner. Most people know that. Yet even in apparently happy marriages someone will sometimes stray, 'play away from home' as the euphemism goes. It is one of the few nuclear buttons and yet those in marriages press it. As a priest one hears often, 'I don't know why I did it.' Part of the temptation may just be that it is forbidden. Freedom of choice is deeply tempting, even when the freedom will have self-destroying results. Not to exercise the freedom of choice requires sacrifice.

Reconciliation is always costly. It can only begin by one side seeking to break the log-jam that is destructive conflict. Almost invariably that will need to be the stronger party. Morally, it should be in most circumstances one can imagine. The need for mercy and for a willingness to give something up in order to be reconciled is spoken of by Jesus in a parable in the Gospel of Matthew (18.23-35). Jesus is telling about the just rule of God, what he calls the kingdom of Heaven, and describing what it is to experience such rule. He tells of two servants. The first owes their mutual master a vast sum of money, more than he could ever repay. The master is sorting out his finances, sends for the slave and tells him that if he does not repay his debt he will be put in prison with his family. The slave begs for mercy and the master relieves him of the debt. The second slave owes the first a pitiful sum. But, after having been forgiven the huge debt by the master, the first slave proves to be merciless and has the second slave imprisoned. The master hears of it, and reverses the mercy shown to the first for failing to follow his example.

There are many ways of looking at this story and many meanings to it. Within it there is a pattern of reconciliation. Debt is a burden, for many an intolerable one. It is another way of translating the word used for trespasses in the Lord's Prayer, so that it would be perfectly valid to pray, instead of '*trespasses*', 'Forgive us our *debts*, in the same way as we forgive those *indebted* to us.' The paying off of debts to someone is one way of making a relationship more even. Right through the Old Testament, debt is seen as a loss of liberty, and the creditor who is ruthless in demanding repayment or foreclosing on security taken from the poor is seen as deeply wicked. Those to whom I owe a debt have power over me. Being a creditor is powerful, being a debtor involves taking on weakness and worry.

Many of us have experienced these pressures in our own lives. The day a home mortgage or loan is paid off is a day of liberation. One of the greatest burdens in many societies is debt slavery. In the UK it can come from losing a job and racking up debts to a high-interest lender or on credit cards. In many countries subsistence farmers borrow money to pay for seed and repay it from the proceeds of harvest, at high rates of interest. Natural disaster or family illness preventing work leaves them literally enslaved, unable to make any decisions for themselves. In its turn that leads to the breakdown of community relationships with lenders, often themselves farmers with more land or capital.

Who can start the process of forgiveness that leads to reconciliation? It must be the more powerful person being willing to make a sacrifice. In Jesus' story it starts with the master, who sets a pattern of reconciliation through debt forgiveness. The first slave cannot be reconciled to the master by his own efforts because he has no equivalent resource. The first slave commits the sin of not himself sacrificing his power and exercising the same justice so as to be reconciled to the second.

Both the master and the first slave need to make a sacrifice. Until they have decided to do that, the situation is only resolvable by destructive conflict in which the weaker party must lose, and all future relationship is impossible. Of course, the sacrifice by itself is not the end. It starts a process. Self-sacrifice without genuine and equal relationships leads to another form of debt: a sense of resentment at being helped.

This parable opens the way to thinking about two aspects of reconciliation. First, it is liberation for all involved. Liberation may not change the fundamental situation, but it transforms the potential. In the parable the slaves remain enslaved, the reality for about one-third of the population of the time. The parable is not about the evils of slavery. Yet their enslavement will be changed over time by the fact that they should have had an opportunity not to be debtors.

A modern historical parallel is in the outcomes of the peace process in Europe in 1919 at the Treaty of Versailles and in 1945 after the unconditional surrender of Germany. Both were complicated and the second was not completed until the Charter of Paris for a New Europe in 1990, which effectively ended the first Cold War. The largest question in 1919 and 1945 was what to do with the defeated Germany, by far the weakest power.

In 1919 the decision was to impose severe demands for reparations and to take many other steps to ensure that

Germany remained weak. After four years of world war the desire for revenge was understandable but its impact was disastrous. The German economy of the Weimar Republic remained hobbled by debt in a way that damaged its society. John Maynard Keynes began his celebrated career by resigning from the UK Treasury staff working on the treaty and writing *The Economic Consequences of the Peace*, in which he forecast disaster as a result of the economic and social impact of reparations.

By contrast in 1946, led by the Americans, there was a clear intention on the part of the western allies to enable Germany to remain united and to minimize or avoid reparations. The Soviet Union took a different view. However, after much struggle the decision of the western powers at least was to readmit Germany (or West Germany, at least) to the family of nations. The debts of the Third Reich were written off. Reparations were relatively slight. There was no revenge taken except in judicial terms for war crimes. The result, when combined with the establishment of an iron and steel pact and then the Common Market, has led to the longest sustained period of peace in western Europe since the fall of the Roman Empire.

That does not mean competition has ended or that friction has stopped. It did not mean that hatred evaporated overnight. It did not provide cover for the atrocities committed by Germany in the Second World War. In brief, it did not make everything 'all right' as though conflict can be reconciled as easily as a child can be stopped crying by being picked up and cuddled.

The process of reconciliation, which is almost eternal and needs constant renewal, required vast sacrifice by the victors in the war. They had to surrender the desire for revenge. They had to resist the urge to break up and deindustrialize a nation that, in the case of France, had been their opponent in three appalling wars within seventy-five years, in each of which France had suffered terribly. In the case of the USA the sacrifice involved the Marshall Plan to prevent the final collapse of the German and western European economies. The UK needed to find the means to forgive and to aid its former enemy.

Reconciliation is costly economically but also psychologically and, again, it is almost always the more powerful party that must sacrifice the most psychologically, above all their sense of domination. Christian understanding is that the source of reconciliation, the spring from which it flows into all the world, is the boundless and generous mercy of God revealed through the birth, life, suffering, crucifixion, resurrection and ascension of Jesus Christ. The key point is that almost every understanding of divine reconciliation involves the notion of some idea of sacrifice.[1]

In other words, for God to be reconciled with human beings, God needed to initiate reconciliation and to demonstrate that God is serious about it. The 'seriousness' of God's sacrifice reveals at the same time the abundant love and determination of God and the abundant peril of living without reconciliation. In John's Gospel 3.16 either John or Jesus says: 'For God so loved the world that he gave his only Son, so that anyone who believed in him should not perish but have eternal life.' It is because reconciliation matters so much that it requires sacrifice, a principle in both divine and human practice at all levels.

Sacrifice is a problem first, because most people are often in favour of the nobility of other people's sacrifice but not their own. That is especially true when the impact of sacrifice is very rarely effective unless it is by the stronger person or group. Take, at one extreme, the issue of the proliferation of nuclear weapons. If the UK or France forewent owning them, or even committed to a no-first-use or sole-purpose condition on their use, the international impact is unlikely to be more than marginal. If China, Russia or the USA did the same then there would be a very high chance of a breakthrough in new treaties.

In litigation between unequal parties, for example a shop that uses a name, and has used it for a long time, which is being sued for trademark infringement by a major international company that has a similar brand, the generosity of the latter will bring reconciliation, whereas concession by the former will simply be seen as bowing to the inevitable.

The difficulty is that the powerful have become so by avoiding concessions when they are in a position of advantage. Sacrifice demands that they take a different attitude, even acquire a new heart towards the weak.

Sacrifice is a problem, second, because of timing differentials: the fruits of reconciliation take time, the costs of sacrifice are immediate. Jesus had to die before he could be raised. The early apostles were martyred generations before the Church became a force to be reckoned with. Sacrifice takes risk and requires faith. In a bitterly fought divorce, the husband might be advised that, as he is wealthy and his wife not and as he has a strong legal position for reasons to do with the case, he should make it clear that he will fight every inch of the way in the courts. Yet, if he wants reconciliation, which may not involve the continuation of the marriage but may possibly leave the relationships able to be healed and the children less traumatized, he might decide to offer to submit to mediation. The risk is immediate, the probability is that he will do less well in the short term, but in the long term it may be that the children, even his wife, will feel a deep sense of gratitude for the sacrifice. It is a hard choice.

HONOUR AND SHAME

We don't talk much about honour in the Global North nowadays, although shame is still a word much in use. However, honour and shame remain influential in the way we relate to others individually and collectively.

Football is a classic example, much studied by sociologists. In cities like Liverpool, which has two historic and stand-out teams, the mood of the whole city is lifted or lowered by the results of the teams. Some signs are sinister, domestic violence rises sharply after a defeat. The same happens nationally when a country's team is defeated. Others are inspiring, the whole community becomes a better place when one team is doing well, and when that's true of both there is magic in the air. It may be that the word respect is substituted for honour, but the impact is the same. Collectively there is a sense of honour. When the team loses there is a sense of shame.

Shame brings anger, a turning inwards and a blame culture. 'Shame is the experience of one's felt sense of self-disintegration in relation to a dysregulating other.'[2] In Lucie Lunn's and other papers it is argued that, first, all human beings are somewhere on a spectrum of shame and that there is not an opposite, although dignity is what might be described as an antidote. Second, she sees shame as intrinsically linked to language. Third, that the experience of corporate shame is linked to individual experience and that empathy from a member of a group that has had shame projected onto it through the use of language may result in anger at perceived injustice even if perpetrated by a person's own group, rather than joining in corporate shame.

The first view is very much that of many psychologists. Shame is not guilt. Guilt in Christian thinking opens the way to repentance and forgiveness and thus to reconciliation with God. It implies responsibility, accountability or even personal action or omission. Guilt and shame are often blurred, but the latter tends to be destructive, alienating us from others and leading to lies, not reconciliation. The former turns us outwards to see the victim or object of our wrongdoing and to desire reconciliation and reparation for the harm done. It is summed up perfectly and economically in the Church of England's Book of Common Prayer confession:

> Almighty and most merciful Father, We have erred, and strayed from thy ways like lost sheep, We have followed too much the devices and desires of our own hearts, We have offended against thy holy laws, We have left undone those things which we ought to have done, And we have done those things which we ought not to have done, And there is no health in us: But thou, O Lord, have mercy upon us miserable offenders; Spare thou them, O God, which confess their faults, Restore thou them that are penitent, According to thy promises declared unto mankind in Christ Jesu our Lord: And grant, O most merciful Father, for his sake, That we may hereafter live a godly, righteous, and sober life, To the glory of thy holy Name. Amen.

In the Communion service according to the Book of Common Prayer the congregation acknowledge their sins and say, 'the burden of them is intolerable'. Bunyan's *Pilgrim's Progress* pictures guilt as a great backpack of enormous weight that hinders all that we do. In his book, the Pilgrim takes the burden up a steep hill topped with three crosses, and at the foot of the central cross, when he kneels, it falls off his back and rolls down the hill.

Shame is different. It comes upon us unawares, externally or internally. It is more like a hidden cancer that weakens us, hindering like guilt, but without the same objective and healthy incentive to seek forgiveness.

Shame is a weapon used very often by the strong against the weak. Whether it is through being gaslighted,[3] through harassment and bullying, through sexual or other forms of abuse, or through collective social action in dysfunctional organizations and societies, shame may be imposed. Victims may know that they are not to blame yet feel shame.

In this view shame is always destructive and negative as well as being mainly individual. In most levels of reconciliation one of the hardest barriers to break down is the individual against the collective.

The question is, does shame have a role in triggering reconciliation? There is an argument that it creates space by enabling a group to identify itself more clearly and to respond to the identification by collectively seeking reconciliation to mitigate the shame. In this view, collective shame is more like guilt and exists as a trigger to do the right thing.

Here the psychology and sociology differ. The former tends to look individually and the latter collectively.

I will come back to the issue in reconciliation after looking at honour.

Honour historically and in the Bible enhanced risk taking, gave courage and hope, led to flights of imagination and joyful generosity. Honour was something perceived externally, applying mainly to men and received by the individual: 'they shall learn I am just the man they take me for'[4] was a characteristic ambition. The weight of preserving honour for women was very heavy. In patriarchal societies they were expected to demonstrate virtue, and even when they were victims of sexual violence they were perceived as shamed. That legacy continues indirectly today even in countries like the UK but very much so elsewhere.

What makes us respected? For many it is honour. What enables our names to live on beyond our bodies? Again, honour. For thousands of years that has been one of the priorities in human existence, especially among men in positions of power. There are more than two hundred mentions of honour in the Bible. In the Psalms, kings pray for honour from God, they honour God with worship, they trust that God will honour them.

One book, that of Esther, is in part a description of competition for honour. The king in Babylon divorces his queen for failing to show him honour. After a search by courtiers, he finds a new queen – a Jewish woman called Esther, of great beauty – who becomes his wife. One of the king's advisers, Haman, plots to have the Jews massacred across the Empire. Esther's uncle, Mordecai, persuades her to intercede with the king, a risky undertaking, as to approach the king without invitation was to risk the sentence of death. However, after some hesitation she acts and invites him to two banquets, using food and beauty (it is a story of great humour, almost slapstick, and political intrigue). The tables are turned. The wicked Haman is shamed, Mordecai is honoured, and the Jews are saved. The events are still celebrated at the feast of Purim in the Jewish calendar.

The theme of honour is particularly relevant to the men. The king has honour because he is king, although the story shows him to be a bit slow of thought and open to manipulation. Haman seeks honour by serving the king. He aims to shame the Jews and gain honour for himself. Mordecai is humble, sitting at the gate, but a decisive leader with a clear sense of the providence of God. He is faithful in protecting the king and seeks protection for the Jews through the protection of God indicated by the high favour in which Esther is held.

Honour is not the same as pride, nor shame as humility. Haman is proud but without honour from the king and ultimately is executed. Mordecai is humble but receives honour when his service is recognized by the king.

This sort of bestowed honour/shame culture has been predominant in most societies in most periods. Even in the UK to this day, the awards given to distinguished people are called 'honours' and at the award ceremony the monarch 'honours' the recipient.

In past times, until certainly the early period of the twentieth century, honour was a legitimate reason for pride. An ancient name, a long-standing title, great wealth inherited, gave honour 'with no damned nonsense about merit' as the British prime minister Lord Melbourne remarked about being made a Knight of the Garter.

Honour is indeed often unlinked to merit. In many societies important people have honour that they cannot lose unless they are caught out in ill-doing in a way that is shameful. Bribery and corruption may be prevalent, but if they are linked to historic and cultural approaches to honour, such as support of dependants, clan or tribe, the support given enhances honour. Abuse of wealth for purely personal gain rather than as a sign of collective honour for those associated with the leader may bring shame and anger, but if it demonstrates importance and wealth it is a matter of praise.

In Homer's *Iliad* the origin of the Trojan War is the slight to the honour of King Agamemnon when the Trojan prince, Paris, steals his beautiful wife, Helen. War was considered by the ancient Greeks as a way of gaining honour, and perceived cowardice in war brought shame on the person, on their family and on their army if they were a leader.

The issues of honour and shame are still with us, although often in countries like the UK they are implicit. To some extent they are being revived through social media. Shaming is easy through anonymous posts. The power of the written word can circle the globe faster than Puck in *A Midsummer Night's Dream*.[5] Honour still carries a leader far even when unmerited; shame can topple a saint and not be revealed to be false for years. Shame can cripple the will and turn the mind inwards. It can divide a group that is able to do good and remove the courage to act at all. One of the great dangers to free speech and honest expression of views is the fear of being attacked and shamed with accusations impossible to disprove.

Courage and honour are linked. Shame has the psychological effect of triggering depression and undermining courage. To say or do anything becomes impossible. Being honoured restores courage and courage leads to acting honourably.

Neurochemistry and Remembering
the Body

The third hindrance is what happens other than in the thinking process. We are not minds alone, but bodies, and even our minds are driven to some degree by chemistry and hormonal reactions with the release of chemicals in response to stimuli. The sight of a threat or the sense that one is about to emerge stimulates the fight-or-flight response. Had you been a hunter-gatherer thousands of years ago that might have been useful, but if you are sitting in a meeting seeking to negotiate a way forward it is likely to provoke unhelpful responses.

Yet we forget this so easily. I am aware that the surroundings in which a mediation is held will have a material impact on the outcome. A windowless room with poor air conditioning will lead to arguments and obstinacy. A good view, adequate refreshments and breaks to get energy back opens minds to new possibilities. The reading list at the end of this book explores the neurochemistry more adequately than I am able to do. It is clear that prolonged exposure to conflict, especially to violence that can be perceived as risking life, alters the entire way in which the mind and body work. Illness is more frequent. Rationality diminishes. Impulsive behaviour becomes more likely. At some point even the DNA is changed.

Worse still is when the experience of fear-filled lives passes from one generation to another. This may be the experience of those in countries like the South Sudan where no generation has lived in peace since the 1950s or even before. Or it may be in a family or a community where habitual dysfunctionality becomes part of the way things are done and the experience of new generations is long-term impacts on mental health for physiological as much as emotional reasons.

The pattern of the ministry of Jesus is of body, mind and soul. When he raises to life the dead daughter of a synagogue leader in Mark 5, he ensures her privacy, treats her gently, and ensures that she is given something to eat.

In a meeting in June 2021, one of the presenters started memorably with the phrase, 'remember the body'. Reconciliation is deeply hindered when we forget that we are bodies and minds, wills and reactions. This section is short, because I am not sufficiently scientifically qualified to write adequately on the subject. However, it is indispensable to consider the psychology, the neurochemistry and the bodily aspects of reconciliation. As will be seen in the next part of the book, handling the issues raised by the body is part of the reconciling process. It is another area that demands partnerships to work on reconciliation, as discussed in Part II.

Always Complete the Course

Most people who have regular access to antibiotics are aware of the instructions on the label, 'always complete the course'. Normally, with most routine infections, after a couple of days one feels much better. The temptation is to stop taking the tablets. But the result of doing so before the course is complete is that the infection is likely to return in much greater strength.

Reconciliation takes a very long time and to some extent is treatment for the chronic diseases of power seeking, of relationship breakdown and of the desire to dominate that so easily becomes part of the human condition.

Reconciliation is a combination of treatments. Mediation may enable a ceasefire or calm a community quarrel enough for longer-term work on meeting, rebuilding relationships and further mediation focused on the underlying issues.

The greatest danger is to think something is complete and to cease to pay attention to the issues that make differences so hard to handle. The *Difference Course*, described and discussed in Part III, is focused on habits, not meetings. It is through cultivating the characteristics of being a reconciled reconciler that long-term means of facing disagreement well can be built.

SUMMARY

- Reconciliation is hard because of the hardness of the human heart and the immediacy of the challenges it offers as against the delayed but far greater rewards it brings.
- It requires sacrifice by those who have an advantage and can thus see the hope of victory as more attractive than the hard work of reconciling relationships.
- It is generally hindered by feelings of shame, but helped by a transparent recognition of guilt. Honour and shame are often unhelpful in that they are not always built on virtue and vice but frequently on perception.
- Remember the body.
- Take time, complete the course.

POINTS TO PONDER

- Think of a conflict you know, anything from family to climate change. Who is the stronger party? What sacrifice would move things forward a little? What can you do to help?
- Is honour/shame an issue in your life or those around you? What does it look like in your own culture or society?
- What physical conditions makes you prone to destructive quarrels? What are the ways in a community or parish of remembering the body?
- Think of an example of reconciliation. Is it ever finished? If so, what would finished look like and how could you tell?

Biblical Reflection

1 Corinthians 1.10-18 and 2 Corinthians 5.17-21. Two letters to the same church, a church that gave Paul much heartache.

- From 1 Corinthians 1, what do you imagine the life of the Corinthian church was like? Is it the sort of church you would have been pleased to go to? What was going wrong? What was Paul's first response?
- From 2 Corinthians, what is the call of God to Christians? What does an ambassador do? What does it tell us about God and ourselves that such a muddled church can still hope to be ambassadors?

3

Changing the Heart

If the obstacles to peacebuilding and reconciliation are so severe, what hope is there? Where is it possible to find the resources to overcome the inertia, the wickedness, the rackets and power games, the deep-set structures of evil – the principalities and powers as St Paul calls them in chapter 6 of his epistle to the Ephesians – that come together to overwhelm the weak, the unthinking and the negligent?

As in looking at the obstacles, this chapter does not pretend to be the volumes-long work that would be necessary to explore all the resources for peacebuilding. I will try to look at some examples and pick up some attitudes that provide a grounding. Parts II and III of this book will develop that thinking and apply it.

THE MORAL IMAGINATION

In the early 2000s I was invited to facilitate a gathering in Bujumbura, the capital of Burundi, where government and opposition military and politicians would discuss reconciliation. The long civil war in Burundi that had started around the time of the Rwandan Genocide, more than ten years earlier, had died down to some extent as a result of ceasefires. Travel was still complicated, and flare-ups were frequent.

The meeting was held in a hotel. Around thirty attended for three days of discussion, all in French. There was a very suspicious atmosphere as long-term enemies met. On the third day a senior government military officer pointed across the room and said, 'That man's militia killed 30,000 people. How can I be reconciled?'

We were near Lake Tanganyika and I pointed out of the window to the beautiful sight of the lake and hills.

'If you go out in a boat and fall into the water, what do you do?'
'Swim!' came the answer.
'And if you can't swim?'
'Then you drown.'
'And if you do not find a way to reconcile then you will all die.'

The last chapter set out just a few of the issues of reconciliation. It is easy to conclude that peacebuilding is impossible. At its heart is the need for a leap of moral imagination[1] towards a possibility previously unimaginable, a structure for peaceful and reconciled disagreement that is radically different from the experience of destructive conflict. This is the point where an outsider may help. Peacebuilding in many conflicts at any level may seem so impossible that the only response is to continue fighting.

John Lederach comments:

> The moral imagination proposes that turning points and
> a journey towards a new horizon are possible, though
> based on perplexing paradoxes. The turning points
> must find a way to transcend the cycles of destructive
> violence while living with and being relevant to the
> context that produces those cycles. A horizon, though
> visible, is permanently just out of touch, suggesting an
> epic journey, the pursuit of which in peacebuilding,
> is the forging of new ways to approach human affairs
> with an enemy.[2]

That is what is meant by moral imagination: it leads to a
change of heart. In all sorts of conflict, the aim becomes
more and more towards winning, even when winning
is an empty dream. Whether it is a family arguing over
an inheritance, or a group seeking political power in a
country, once the conflict – within its own context –
becomes destructive then only change of heart and a
new imagination gives the strength to move forward.
The very act of planning victory is itself one sort of
imagination that energizes and motivates those involved
even where the consequences of victory, let alone defeat,
would be terrible.

In March 2021, the UK government published a review
of the outlook for security, defence and development
in the 2020s.[3] It is a powerful and comprehensive
document, probably the widest ranging of its kind in
very many decades, possibly ever. Yet in many places it
suffers from a lack of moral imagination, especially in
dealing with world-changing threats like nuclear war.
It includes an approach to nuclear warfare strategy, but

never asks the question about consequences. If there was a nuclear war and the UK deployed and used its weapons, what happens next? It comes in the category of 'too difficult, ignore'.

Such a failure of the necessary imagination of the moral consequences of proposed actions are typical of conflicts that pursue a single, straight road, well paved with good intentions. Its underlying assumption is that 'we can control events', 'we will win', or 'it won't happen'. Yet all the history of wars reveals that they are times of chaos and error, where often the side that makes the fewer mistakes wins.

The same is true of domestic or community quarrels. Where the whole resources of imagination are taken up with seeking to win and with mulling over the horrible nature of the enemy, no space, no bandwidth, is left for the moral imagination. The long, straight and well-paved road is never looked at afresh with the question, 'Can I or we imagine an alternative, a fork in the road that takes us on the hard and stony path of peace?'

Lederach quotes his researcher as writing: 'In our context of thirty plus years of the Troubles [in Northern Ireland], violence, fear and division are known. Peace is the mystery! ... Peace is Mystery. It is walking into the unknown.'[4]

The first and indispensable resource for overcoming a sense that conflict is inexorable, unavoidable, conquering all the best intentions, is the moral imagination. The moral imagination is the responsibility of leadership. It is perhaps *the* example of leadership that most clearly sets great leaders apart.

In the twentieth century there are many examples of such moral imagination. In Chapter 1, I have already referred to the leadership of those who sought to bring western Europe together after 1945, to provide a pathway for peaceful competition and to end the centuries of terrible wars that had killed so many, especially since 1870. There are many more examples. After the Nigerian Civil War of 1967–70, President Gowon of Nigeria declared, 'no victors, no vanquished', and thereby started a process of reconciliation that has endured to some extent for half a century. After the fall of the Berlin Wall in 1989, Germany was reunited, and other countries in the former communist-ruled centre and east of Europe adjusted in largely peaceful revolutions. In what was then Czechoslovakia, President Václav Havel, a former political prisoner, led the country into peaceful adjustment (the Velvet Revolution of 1989) and then into the 'velvet divorce' when in 1993 Slovakia separated and received independence. In February 1990, following his twenty-seven years of imprisonment, soon-to-be-president Nelson Mandela navigated the transition to Black majority rule in South Africa, along with President de Klerk.

There are many quibbles and many serious objections that can be raised with every example. None of them demonstrates a process of moral imagination that is eternal or that became part of the DNA of a country or a movement. Time goes by, the vision of the founders fades. Others replace them, the pain of conflict is forgotten as the generation that lived it grows old and dies. Moral imagination, like forgiveness, is a fragile plant that needs constant attention. Moral imagination never will be in human DNA: our desires for power, our capacity to find enemies, our pride and foolish self-reliance, all prevent such a deep change in human nature.

But when it flowers, miracles happen. That fragile plant will, for a few years or even a couple of generations, shelter nations from war and turn human hearts to love for those with less resources than them. Its flowering can be renewed with the right leaders and the right inspiration.

Inspiration matters at several levels. It is far more than emotional. It affects perception and influences imagination. It can change the attitude to outgroups by members of an opposed ingroup. It works across the whole human being,[5] including in the neurochemistry that has a powerful influence on emotions, on decision-making capacity, on ethical attitudes. Inspiration changes perceptions of challenges or, to put it another way, it can nourish or restrict the moral imagination. Studies have shown that perceptions of a challenge, such as climbing a very steep hill, will be improved if someone has a positive and confident companion – the hill, in the case of the climber, then being physically perceived as less steep. Perceptions of threat are appropriate when facing someone violent or for a fighter in battle, but they pose dangers to peace negotiations. Inspiration may nurture a different attitude.

The first and most important resource in peacebuilding is the moral imagination described above: nobody will retain that imagination without being nurtured and inspired by leadership and by functional and mutually supportive communities. Reconciliation is seldom, if ever, the choice of a lone individual and even if they make that choice, they still need the resilience and persistence that comes from community.

A Holistic Focus

The second key resource is a holistic approach to building peace. Peacebuilding is very often seen as those things that capture the headlines. Prime ministers and presidents come and go in convoys of armoured vehicles and howling sirens. They are surrounded by people in dark glasses with curly wires coming out of their ears who talk to their shirt cuffs and are always looking for threats. Exhausted spokespeople talk of honest discussions, slow progress, hope of a breakthrough or the achievement of settlement. Signings are held in large halls with people passing documents from one to the other and pens being exchanged. Polling figures are consulted to see what the impact has been on re-election chances.

Then the caravan moves on. Three or five or seven years later, the struggle re-emerges, perhaps a little different but always the same basic virus of violence. Nobel Prizes are not returned, the politicians may have moved on, but the people, the sufferers, the women raped, the men ignored, were never touched. They had a few courses on job finding, but their hearts and intentions were not treated as having the same intrinsic value and independence as those of the leaders, and their moral imagination was neither inspired nor nurtured. The struggle begins again and this time it is worse.

In the sixteenth century, during the French religious wars, a leader on one side commented that 'in the first war we fought like men, in the second like animals and in the third like demons'. Conflict does not improve with age, nor does it decay and become less dangerous. It rots. The rot is poisonous to the body, mind and spirit of the individual and of the society.

Yet there is as much problem with the hidden work that happens. Grassroots groups may work intensely and intelligently. Local efforts may bring local peace. Yet regional conflicts overwhelm as does the pressure of others with a dog in the fight or who are just observers with bias and interests. The leaders call their followers to arms and out of peer pressure and desire for honour the middle-rank leaders and the people at the most local level respond.

Peacebuilding in every situation must be top down, middle out and bottom up, all at once, all linked and all inclusive.

The illustration of the need for a holistic approach is a failure that taught me a lesson. In the early 2000s, the group with whom I worked at Coventry Cathedral was invited to support work on peacebuilding in an area of an African country. It was a border area where historic expansion of Christianity and Islam met. It was also a border between farmers and pastoralists as well as two ethnic groups. Several thousand people had died during clashes. The area was remote, and police and army groups could not reach threatened towns and villages in time. I remember walking through burned-out settlements one Ash Wednesday, the dust and ash rising into the air from the ruins and the humps of shallow graves in the ground. Hostility, deep hatred, were all around.

The process was long but for a while it was effective. Influential people in different villages were given satellite phones so that they could communicate. They were trained a little and had a very few numbers programmed in. Some training on conflict management was given to local police units. If a person with a phone heard that there was trouble brewing, they could phone the equivalent elder in the nearest village from where the trouble might come, or might be going, and warn them. They would also call the police, rather than walking for hours to a place where they could call.

The results were dramatic for a while. There was a good deal of peace and collaboration. Then, at a higher level, the whole region erupted into new violence and in a short period all the progress was swept away. We had supported the real reconcilers who were local, and the next level up, the middle. But the top remained untouched. The result was failure to establish sustainable non-violence for long enough to change the moral imagination towards peace.

PARTNERSHIP

Everyone wants the glory. Everyone wants, being human, to be recognized for what they have done. NGOs, whether local or international, rely on attention to maintain access to funding streams. Having led an NGO within Coventry Cathedral, I remember well the pressure. It is not corruption or greed, merely the normal reality that any institution seeks to preserve its own life, and, in most institutions, 'life' is represented by money to carry out work. Without money, staff cannot be kept and new projects cannot be completed. In one sense this is right. A good organization, with visionary ideas, comes into being and grows. Sooner or later, however, its initial vision and sharpness of aims and values are blurred as people come to work for it who were not there at the beginning. As it gets larger, more time is spent on finance and function and less on the front line.

Equally, no institution is capable of doing all that is needed. Those with skills at mediation may well not be so good at running refugee or IDP[6] settlements. There may be very severe problems of security that require working with peacekeeping or peacemaking organizations. Epidemics will need medical support. Displaced and disturbed children will need education and stability. Many of all ages and types will require trauma counselling. There will be the need of resettlement, of rebuilding an economy with microfinance and other support. The list is endless.

Perhaps the most difficult and most valuable part of putting together an effort in reconciliation is assembling a team and having the humility or ethos among its members to be willing to share the way forward.

In the UK a town was divided by prospects of a new motorway running close by. The route would divide it from other, smaller villages in the community, and there would be more noise and a disturbance to the view. Many of the older and more conservative households were against it. They had settled in the area towards the end of their working lives, mostly professional and white-collar elite, and they resented the change to the character of the area. For exactly the same reasons, a minority of the older people, those who had grown up there and to quote someone I knew, 'their grandparents are in the churchyard', were in favour because their children could not afford the increasingly expensive housing and would have to move away. For some others, who came from families in the area for up to seven generations, this felt like the end of the world.

The community needed better facilities and affordable housing, not a road.

The priest of the parish rather naively invited people to an open meeting at the church to discuss a way forward. Ahead of the date both sides, who had representatives on the town council, agreed who would speak and a line to take. The meeting quickly turned not into a debate but into an exchange of explosive-filled speeches that did not attempt to address the fears of the other but were aimed at rallying hard-line support for their own view.

The parish priest put aside her fantasies of being loved by everyone because she had put the community back together, and with considerable courage picked herself up and got advice.

To cut the story of a couple of years very short, she found partners and, with a group, mapped the conflict. They saw who had what interests, who led them and who encouraged them. They listened carefully and built relationships with different groups, not least with church services tailored for every different group. They worked with small groups, trained people in listening skills and in having difficult conversations. They understood some very physical needs, such as for improved surgeries, a bigger school and better and cheaper shopping. By the end they had enabled the majority, but not all, of the community to accept that the motorway could go ahead, and negotiated with developers that the new jobs it would bring as transport links improved would open the way to new housing that was appropriate for the area and affordable for those who would work there. There would be more shopping, a sports centre and a new secondary school.

They did not live happily ever after, and the priest was not loved by everyone, until the next one came, when, of course, the previous one was seen as a golden age, but the community grew in diversity and functioned as a place of welcome and hope. And that is good enough.

Think about what was needed for that outcome. Mediation and reconciliation were only part of the problem. There needed to be social understanding, training, developers, lawyers, educationalists, doctors and loads of volunteers. Scale it up to a violent conflict over a region and the complexity grows enormously. Scale it globally and face an issue like climate change and it is orders of magnitude more complex still.

It is obvious that at almost no level can things be done alone. Even a single household may well need mediation, counselling, financial advice, support for a bullied child at school and help to get a leaking roof repaired. The key issue for anyone involved in mediation and reconciliation work is to know what they can do and to ensure that the right team is assembled. We will look at how this is done more carefully in Part II.

A Commitment to Truth and Transparency

At UK schools, textbooks in history usually describe the Battle of Trafalgar as the key naval engagement of the Revolutionary and Napoleonic Wars in which the Royal Navy defeated a stronger Franco-Spanish force after a dramatic chase across the Atlantic and back. It is set out as the moment that stopped Napoleon's 'Army of England' mounting an invasion. The next passage will usually say that the army at Boulogne then broke camp and marched across Europe to defeat the

Dual Monarchy at Ulm and Austerlitz and in 1806 the Prussians at Jena. Nelson's death is always painted in heroic colours. The Royal Navy celebrates Trafalgar Day (21 October) with dinners and a toast to 'the immortal memory'.

A French history textbook for schools described Trafalgar as a naval engagement off the Spanish coast in which the British admiral was killed. End of story.

Both statements are true, but neither is the whole truth. The understanding of history is seldom precise. There is always a myth that somehow 'truth' in a dispute exists somewhere. The reality is that the nature of conflict at all levels of our lives makes us perceive reality differently. There is a letter in our family from someone who was part of the Charge of the Light Brigade in 1854 at the Battle of Balaclava in the Crimean War. It was written to his mother immediately after the battle. He tells of the charge, of friends who were killed or wounded, and of his horse having been hit by a shell splinter. Surely this would be accurate? It certainly is, but it is only one aspect of the battle and contradicts other accounts in some important ways. There is a true account of the battle, but no single person could tell it and no history will get every detail right.

We all have the experience of listening to friends whose marriage or relationship has broken down. It is painful and sad. It is also confusing. Sometimes there is a sort of resigned defeatism, 'it just was not working', which cannot be explained. Sometimes there are flat contradictions. The outsider cannot tell which is true and often even those involved don't know or convince themselves of truth that has no relation to what happened. Finding the truth is a difficult process, and the bigger the conflict the more complicated the truth. It takes time and often a process of enquiry.

The Truth and Reconciliation Commission (TRC) approach was most famously applied in South Africa after the fall of the Apartheid regime. Chaired by the Anglican Archbishop of Cape Town, Desmond Tutu, it achieved a remarkable success in enabling the hardest of stories to be told by victims and perpetrators. Not only did this result in a far clearer understanding of truth, but in some remarkable cases it opened the way to reconciliation between individuals and symbolized the beginnings of reconciliation for the nation.

TRCs have been tried in many places. The key to their working is a deep commitment to transparency by individuals and organizations. They must have official support and a willingness by all significant figures to be open and not simply to use a TRC as a forum for putting their own case. Truth is only found by transparency that listens as well as speaks. It requires the humility of being able to accept that wrong has been done. Above all, TRCs require leadership that is trusted in the way that both President Mandela and Archbishop Tutu were.

Truth and transparency are painful and costly. A commitment to both is essential but needs help through skilled and trusted figures in a TRC or through good facilitators in other methods. What matters is developing habits of facing conflict in a way that always leaves space for changing of minds. 'My truth, right or wrong' does not lead to progress.

The sign of a commitment to truth and transparency is the seeking of a joint understanding at best, or at least an understanding of the position of the other. To be able to tell the other's story and to give an account of their view, even when disagreement is profound, is a major step on the journey of reconciliation.

EMBRACE COMPLEXITY

I love simplifying things. To look at a complex problem and be able to extract the key elements in a way that is simple feels like a great achievement. I hold strongly to the adage 'KISS', 'keep it simple, stupid!' Complicated problems end up with untidy solutions.

In some areas of work, it is a good rule. The organization of companies or other institutions is better kept as simple as possible. I once worked in a company that relied on matrix management. The theory was fine: that junior employees like me had more than one manager so that all those above knew what was going on. The result was at best disorder and at worst an opportunity to play off one boss against the other. Paper proliferated as people like me tried to tell all those who we thought might be one of our line managers everything they needed to know about everything we were doing.

However, there is no simplifying the human heart. We seldom understand all our own motivations. The wonderful film *Bridge of Spies* with Tom Hanks and Mark Rylance (2015) is about the Cold War in the 1950s. Mark Rylance plays a Russian spy in the USA who is caught and sentenced to death. His lawyer is played by Tom Hanks. Hanks says to Rylance on several occasions, 'You don't seem worried', and the Rylance character replies, 'Would it help?' Most of us are not quite like that. People annoy us and even when we do not show it, we are unsettled by conversations with them. Often, we cannot quite explain it.

Put our own internal complexity into a group and multiply it by the number of people. Add in the soup of not-quite-understood history and the impact of historic myths and legends. Add a garnish of fear and anxiety for the future, of apprehension for one's family and stability and the ambitions of many leaders. Combine with the influence of those who gain from conflict at all levels. Don't forget the impact of pride and unwillingness to agree one is wrong and the strength of greed for gain and the fruit of victory. Even then one is not anywhere close to the complexity of many conflicts.

Imagine you end up in hospital after you have had a bad fall. You are wheeled into the emergency department. A doctor takes a very quick look and says, 'You have a bruised head; take some paracetamol and lie down until you feel better' but ignores your broken leg. You would not be impressed. You would certainly not get better.

Simplifying the genuinely complex leads not only to misdiagnosis of the problem but also to the wrong treatment and thus no recovery.

A clear example of this is the use of religion or immigration or another single issue as a political hook, on which politicians often hang much more complicated problems. Religion and immigration are easily identifiable differences between people. News and media will often present a conflict as 'religious', or 'tribal', or a similar term. The reality will be a very complicated mixture of history, economics, ethnicity and numerous other causes. For a political leader seeking office, simplification enables more followers to be found. For a reporter in a war zone, who usually understands how intricate the problem is, the pressure of condensing a report into less than two minutes makes complexity impossible to communicate. For someone facilitating the process or for the parties there are no excuses: complexity has to be faced. You cannot heal what you have not identified.

In 2002, I had the privilege of being the note taker at a meeting in Jerusalem chaired by the then Archbishop of Canterbury, George Carey (now Lord Carey). It was a gathering of religious and political leaders who had signed the Alexandria Declaration on religious peace in the Holy Land. There were about twenty-five people present in a brilliantly chaired and fiercely argued meeting. The discussion covered the situation of the *intifada* (the uprising) that was currently happening, the issue of bombings, Jewish and Christian and Islamic theology, as well as a multitude of historic events as far back as the destruction of Herod's Temple in 70 CE. I was sitting next to the British Consul General in Jerusalem, who at one point muttered, 'I hope you understand all this, because I don't.'

No simplification could do justice to the complexity of a dispute that in some readings goes back to the time of Moses. Lord Carey's remarkable ability to hold the subtleties delicately enabled a good outcome to the day. He recognized and embraced the complexity.

Summary

- In some ways the keys to progress come down to character.

- Humility enables partnerships to work, complexity to be embraced and the unknowable and undiscernible aspects of truth to be left on the table where they can be examined over time. Pride seeks self-glory, wants partners only as subordinates, simplifies to show sharp insight and is impatient.
- Openness to others stimulates the moral imagination. A gentle manner and a confidence when needed, another way of saying courage, combine to make it possible for the moral imagination to be spread and taken on board by those in a dispute.
- And I would say faith enables us to call out to the God of peace for blessing on the journey of reconciliation and the miracle of roadblocks circumvented and barriers overcome.

Points to Ponder

- Do you believe reconciliation is possible? Looking back at Part I, are the obstacles too great? List some disputes you have known, locally, in families or on a wider scale. What proportion have been fought out and which ones have shown some fruit of reconciliation? What made the difference?
- What is most discouraging and most encouraging about this Part? Why?
- In your own faith tradition or non-faith tradition, what are the stories that call you to reconciliation?

Biblical Reflection

John 13.1-20

A famous passage. Spend time talking about the reaction of those involved. What would a foot-washing church look like at every level? Try washing each other's feet, if everyone is happy with that. Then share how you feel. Then pray.

PART II

INTRODUCTION

Peacebuilding is about the heart. There is never a *technique* that provides all the answers, but there can be systematic approaches that improve the chances of the people involved in a dispute finding a way forward towards a better outcome. There are also innumerable side-tracks, red herrings and blind alleys that can bring things to a halt.

This Part II is not a method, it is a pattern of working at any level of dispute. It is not exhaustive. It has been helpful. I first came across this pattern when working with Canon Andrew White in Coventry between 2002 and 2005. Later, Canon Paul Oestreicher, Andrew's predecessor in leading the work at Coventry described earlier, confirmed that, although he had not put all of this into words, it was the way he worked.

In the world of peacebuilding and reconciliation there are many very good approaches, often with scientific names and much system. I am not pretending to that. The question is always, 'While lovingly respecting the dignity and autonomy of those in the conflict, what helps them most to find a way to transform destructive conflict into healthy disagreement with diversity and unity held together?'

The Coventry model is based around six words beginning with R. They are not sequential, you don't do one and then the other, but like a juggler you start with one and end with all going at once. That is essential to any peacebuilding. Each R deals with an aspect of being

human and struggling with conflict. To drop or forget one
is to become mechanistic, which always leads to failure.

The underlying principles of the Six Rs are those of
Part I. They are designed to encourage the development
of a holistic approach that draws in partners in the work
of peacebuilding and enables the parties to a dispute to
reimagine the possibility of the 'Mystery of Peace' when
they are accustomed to destructive conflict.

This Part involves the figure of the facilitator, peacemaker
or peacebuilder. I use these words interchangeably to
mean the person – more usually the group of people and
organizations – who seek to enable the parties to find a
way forward in disagreeing well and in rebuilding resilient
and sustainable relationships amid deeply held differences.

In Christian understanding the foundational breakdown
in relationship is that between the creator God and the
human beings who were created and exist to relish and
enjoy relationship with God, each other and the creation,
in a world in which love, righteousness and justice reign.
God's answer is out of love to reconcile human beings
who seek to go their own way, to live independently, to be
autonomous from God. That was done by God becoming
fully human, living a fully human life, dying a fully human
death, in the person of Jesus Christ. He was fully God who
makes all things well, fully human in being tested and
tempted in all things as we are, yet without sin.[1] The core
of Christian belief is that God in Jesus Christ lived with
human suffering, died and rose again to new life, and calls
all people to know God in joy and liberation. In so doing
they find that same new life and the power of God's Spirit
at work in them as the Spirit is already at work in the world.

For Christians not only is the history of Jesus Christ an
example and a pattern to follow, but he also opened the

way to peace with God and to the calling to live as those
who make peace, to be reconciled reconcilers. He is alive
and known, dwelling in us by the Spirit of God given to us.

It was Jesus who said to his disciples, 'Blessed are the
peacemakers for they shall be called children of God.'[2]

All very well, but what does a peacemaker look like?
This part looks at what a peacemaker does, but it also
makes assumptions about character.

At any level of conflict peacemakers are those who stand
in the middle and extend their arms to all, in the way that
Jesus Christ extended his arms on the cross. They become
bridges for people to cross over to embrace those from
whom they have been separated, even hated and in many
cases sought to kill.

Builders of peace are seldom favoured by those with
whom they engage. They are often the lightning conductor
for the rage, fear and despair present in every conflict.
Therefore what are the qualities required?

As this part begins, I will offer two from within
Christian teaching and the pattern of Jesus.

The first is transparency. Peacebuilders are called to be
known. The beautiful passages of the call of the disciples
(John's Gospel, chapter 1) have several questions and
descriptions.

The first is that Jesus is light and in him is no
darkness at all. A characteristic of light is seeing. The
great Christian renewal that began in the 1930s in
East Africa had as one of its rules 'walk in the light' –
especially with those around us. To walk in the light is
to be seen and to see truly. In John 1 the first disciples
ask questions of Jesus, such as 'Where are you staying?'
Jesus replies: 'Come and see.' Nothing is hidden. The
implicit and underlying question addressed to Jesus

that runs through the whole chapter and indeed the whole Gospel is equally simple: 'Who are you?'

Any facilitator of peacebuilding must be knowable and transparent in who they are. Without knowing the facilitator in depth, the participants in a conflict will not be able to trust them. The suspicions of manipulation are almost always so great that the facilitator is assumed to have a hidden agenda in favour of the other parties. Peacebuilders must walk in the light with regards to their own history, their funding and their motivation.

Second, peacebuilders must work in the background. They come to serve; glory is for others. One of the very oldest hymns of the Christian faith is found in the letter to the Philippians, chapter 2. It speaks of Jesus, who did not count equality with God a thing to be grasped, but humbled himself, taking the form of a servant.

The reality is that the people who take the biggest risks in peacebuilding are those who are in conflict. They risk credibility, loss of honour with their followers, being seen as naïve by those siding with them, and so much more. In armed conflicts they risk death at the hands of the more radical. Facilitators do take great risks. For example, the Anglican Communion commemorates every year the Melanesian Martyrs, a group of Melanesian Anglican monks who went to the camp of a warlord in 2003 after a peace agreement ending much of the fighting in the Solomon Islands around the year 2000. They went to plead for peace but were tortured and murdered. In that death for peace is seen the true image of Jesus Christ. They went to serve and were willing to give all.

The temptation to be the hero who makes peace, the centre of the story, is common to many of us. Peacebuilding and facilitating discussions seek something else: the transformation of conflict.

4

Researching or How to Become Consciously Ignorant

We were driving through a swampy area in the Ogoni region of the Niger Delta. It was the original area of oil production in Nigeria, with the first flow in 1956, the same year as my birth. The result of oil is something often referred to as 'the natural resource curse', in which the huge wealth under the ground leads to conflict, to inequality, to corruption and to violence. In the case of Ogoni, to those demons can be added pollution of soil and waterways, destruction of fishing and crops, and deterioration of air quality from the almost uninhibited flaring of the gas that was produced with the oil.

The people who had scarcely – if at all – benefited from the oil that had been produced for fifty years were the local inhabitants. A region that should have looked like Abu Dhabi was still desperately poor, with high underemployment or unemployment, low incomes, short life expectancies and insecurity. Along with militia groups and banditry, life was (and is) insecure.

The outcome has been very understandable unrest. A charismatic leader called Ken Saro-Wiwa founded, with others, the Movement for the Survival of the Ogoni People (MOSOP). In 1995, during the tyrannical, military dictatorship of General Abacha, and with Ogoniland seething with discontent, Ken Saro-Wiwa and some of his colleagues were arrested and then executed by hanging. The company operating the production was Shell. They were accused by MOSOP of collaborating with the government, something they forcefully denied. Additionally, many among the Ogoni people saw the production as the theft of the natural resources and wealth that they should have owned. The unrest meant that oil production had to be shut down. In the early 2000s, Coventry Cathedral's International Centre for Reconciliation was invited to help with a process of reconciliation.

By this time of the closure of the oilfields in the 1990s, Ogoni oil production was somewhat depleted. If oil was to be lifted, each well would produce for a while until the internal pressure dropped and oil stopped flowing. Then the well was closed until the pressure built up again. It was all a bit like the plumbing in old houses.

On that day in Ogoniland, as usual when someone else is driving (I should pay tribute here to my wonderful driver, who went into all kinds of bad places and kept me safe) I was dozing in the hot and humid air blowing through the open windows of the car. A colleague pointed out a steel object rising above the grass at the side of the road. We stopped to take a look at what was a well-head, the kit on the surface of the ground through which oil can be produced, often called a Christmas tree. The metal was in fairly good condition, and despite having been theoretically unused for over ten years, there were fresh, shiny scratches on the top where spanners and wrenches had been used to open it for production. Clearly, oil was being lifted by someone.

As we were looking, we heard voices. A group of about a dozen young men, with machetes but not guns, were standing around the car. They were talking in Ogoni, but when we got near, some began to speak English. They thought we were from Shell and were angry and threatening, speaking of taking us prisoner and asking what we were doing there. They had seen petrol tankers in the area in previous weeks, and assumed Shell were producing oil despite their promises not to. Ogoni could produce, at that time, about 30,000 barrels of high-value crude oil a day and with the price of oil around US$100 for each barrel that was worth doing.

After a while they began to calm down, and we spent quite a long time listening to their stories and their sense of despair at the endless conflict and hopelessness of their lives. Their great refrain was, 'Where has the oil gone?' They also wanted to know why they had not benefited. The conversation ended with a prayer together, and we moved on to the next village and next appointment to listen to others. I was very grateful for the unplanned stop. It offered the chance to hear some voices who were not pre-programmed to lobby us, but spoke from their hearts, albeit very embittered hearts.

The first R is Researching. It is a straightforward list of things to do. Desktop analysis is the beginning: read as much useful information as you can find, which was much less at the time of this story, with the web in its infancy. Look at Twitter feeds, Facebook pages, Instagram, TikTok and the rest. Then interview everyone you can get hold of who is willing to talk. Try and do so in a systematic way, taking notes, and without simply doing a check-list of questions, seeking rather to get things in a shape that enables comparison of stories and discernment of different perspectives. It is much better to do this in pairs. One point to note is that, if at all possible, in cultural areas where that is a sensitivity, women should interview women.

As you interview and listen, the third step is to begin to populate a map of the conflict. This is not a moment of judgement, but simply of analysis. Who are the key parties? Since when have they been involved? Who are and have been the leaders? What is the timeline? What are the key environmental, cultural and other contextual factors? Who are the shadow players with influence but less obvious presence? Who are the spoilers who have a vested interest in the conflict continuing or even getting worse?

I am not going to be prescriptive about tools. This is a book at a general level and specialist publications will be more helpful. An online search will show many different tools for mapping. Like all tools they are only as good as the data that goes into them, so the key to a good map is having covered the ground, metaphorically but preferably sometimes physically. In other words, the map quality depends on the building of a good rapport with those involved directly and listening well. We will look at this more closely in Part III.

Which tool to use will depend on the complexity of the conflict. A tool that could adequately map the Second World War is likely to be a little over the top in a community or family confrontation. At this point I always struggle to hold two things at the same time. The first is to keep the tools used as simple and accessible as possible. There is a well-known but likely apocryphal story from the terrible, long drawn-out struggle in Iraq after the 2003 invasion. The new American general was in place and had asked for a proper conflict map. After some days, there was a presentation with all the possible links and networks. The result covered an entire wall in lines and arrows. The general is said to have remarked that if anyone could understand the map then they would have no trouble with the war.

The best tools will help shape the questions you seek imaginatively but not constrain a flexible response to emerging shapes and patterns that may take the facilitators in new and unexpected directions. In other words, in Lederach's beautiful phrase, they will liberate 'the moral imagination'.[1] Nothing is more important. The experience of researching is often deeply depressing. The move to conscious ignorance is one of recognizing one's position as an outsider, without the same emotional sensitivity as those most closely involved to culture, fear and history. The complexity grows and grows until one's head begins to spin. At first in such situations, I tend to see numerous occasions when it was 'obvious' that the conflict could have been avoided, solved or at least mitigated. As I learn more, I usually feel that there is no solution at all, and that my first reaction left out the emotions of those involved, treating them only as purely rational beings able to separate themselves entirely from emotions. The third step is a more balanced view, aware of ignorance, but also aware of the signs of hope and sensitive to any movement. Humility is an essential.

The moral imagination has to contain room for identification with people who are different, feeling what they feel, even where one disagrees. It cannot be purely distanced and objective. The former is a statement that we are all human beings, the latter is paternalistic. The heart of conflict, whether in a marriage or a war, is an intensification of isolation: those involved think that nobody else can understand and, worse, that nobody else cares. The outsider knows that the first of those two is true but the second can be overcome. There are certain journalists who seem to be able to report well, but always with passion. They do more than tell a story; they conscript the emotions of the hearer. The moral imagination starts with that deep passion for peace, for the well-being of those whose lives are in pain.

The leap of moral imagination is costly and hard, and needs wings on the feet. For example, in the last twenty years the work of interfaith dialogue has been transformed by the use of scriptural reasoning. This involves a group of people learning to study each other's scriptures together. Pursued over time it is not aimed at a syncretistic soup of 'we all really agree' but, through engagement with sacred texts of others, being given the impetus to develop deeper understanding and profound friendships. The sacred writings give wings to the moral imagination.

In any conflict or confrontation, whether it is within a church or school or community, between faiths, or armed struggle at different levels, the facilitator is hearing people's dreams and fears and memories. The loss of a relative in an extrajudicial killing, or the fear that comes from being threatened if one looks too closely at the wrong data or asks the wrong questions or goes to the wrong place, or the despair from seeing one's homeland torn apart, are all areas of emotional horror. One must weep with those who weep.

Even in utterly non-violent situations, dreams and hopes, security and expectations will be in the course of destruction and that leaves people very vulnerable. The worst form of premature judgement is that which says implicitly, 'because this does not much matter to me, I will not allow myself to feel the pain that you are suffering'.

I described a visit to Ogoniland at the beginning of the chapter. That trip was the first step in researching. Much research in a conflict is undramatic. On that occasion we had more drama than usual. We were flown across part of the Niger Delta by Shell, in a helicopter, as they explained to us *their* view of the situation. We spoke to senior managers and those in the middle ranks, a few from Holland, the UK or USA but the vast majority from Nigeria. The conversations were very revealing. Many of the Nigerian staff had family links in Ogoni and felt deeply torn. Some of the expatriates were terrified by their experience of seeking to deal with the problems. We listened to village leaders, women, youths, NGOs, to the very intelligent and passionate Ken Saro-Wiwa Junior and to Ledum Mitee, the man who had succeeded to the leadership of MOSOP after Ken Senior's death. We spoke to people with links to militias, and to crime and corruption. We spoke to Government at numerous levels. The list was very, very long indeed.

What all those meetings did was to reveal complexity. Learned articles by experts in the area spoke of the destruction of the environment and the resulting socio-political impacts. The history of relations with neighbouring ethnic groups and the impact of the Nigerian Civil War (1967–70), where different groups were on different sides, added to the recent historical uncertainty. Then there was that natural resource curse.

Most of the trouble came back to oil and gas. Some of it was linked to the perceived actions of Shell, or their perceived lack of actions. Lawsuits had been started by MOSOP and other groups.[2] There was also significant division among groups in Ogoni and others across the whole oil-producing region, which had resulted in fighting in three states at least. Politics in the region had used oil money gained illegally to fund militias and they had in their turn become drawn into large-scale criminal activity involving kidnapping, drugs and the stealing of vast quantities of oil. Corruption was and remains endemic. Amid it all, those who suffered and suffer the most are the poorest and most vulnerable.

As discussed, earlier researching could be easily termed enquiry. It enables the move from unconscious to conscious ignorance. There are further steps, whether to partial understanding, good understanding or an intuitive grasp of the situation. The reality is that the last of these takes generations. I was listening to a friend who has spent more than forty years in the Democratic Republic of the Congo. He commented that he is beginning to grasp how little he grasps.

Unconscious ignorance is to repeat what 'everyone knows to be true', but almost never is. It is also to take one conflict and project its solution on to another. Unconscious ignorance is the staple fuel for manipulative leadership and for rackets and power games. It is also the staple deception amid well-meaning but damaging intervention, as has been seen in many wars such as Iraq.

Researching muddies the water, or perhaps, to be more exact, it enables one to see that the waters are very muddy indeed. Working through 'what everyone knows' produces simple answers to complicated questions, answers that in reality do not tackle the question at all.

Ogoni is a very good case study. Unconscious ignorance looks at the characteristics of extractive industry conflicts and says, 'It's all the fault of [in this case] Shell.' Or, from another point of view, 'It's all the fault of corrupt government' or militias.

Alternatively, mediators and facilitators of peacebuilding may come in and try to apply the lessons they have learned elsewhere. That sounds sensible but is usually a problem. They may have worked on, or learned from, community/company disputes in Australia, or Papua New Guinea or Latin America. There will of course be lessons but all who work in this area are in danger from time to time of making the problem fit their toolkit rather than getting the tools for the job.

Researching is an interrogative process, not an accusatory one. I make a practice of taking detailed notes of every meeting, so long as those I am meeting give permission. They should be allowed to see what has been written. Taking notes gives a clear sense of being present, and of learning rather than somehow being above those caught up in the situation. Good facilitators are never parachuted in as those who solve, but arrive humbly to serve and assist.

The process of researching is to some extent value neutral. That means that judgement is suspended, at least outwardly, until further stages have been reached. One of the major difficulties is that one deals with bad people. Conflict (even in what is seen as a just cause) brings out the worst in people. It does not matter whether it is in a household or family, or somewhere like Ogoni. All involved are running on their nerves. As was discussed in Chapter 2, the impact of confrontation, especially involving violence and threat of injury or death, is something that builds up responses in the human body. The longer the conflict continues, the stronger those responses become and the weaker the collective impact of moral decision making.

Moral neutrality poses its own dangers. Some of the wickedest people can be the most capable of appearing attractive and helpful, not always deliberately. In many professions, supervision is obligatory. The facilitator or mediator needs accountability to others disconnected from the conflict, in order to see where they are being affected by their contacts. The practitioner shares their experiences and views with someone else, or better still a group. Are they getting too close to a client? Are they being manipulated? Are they allowing proper emotions of humanity and sympathy to colour their approach to others involved? Wise peacebuilders will always have supervision and accountability.

A few years ago I was with a group of very experienced and wise English clergy in Northern Ireland. On one day we met the eloquent and articulate spokespeople for one side. All the clergy came away committed to justice for the oppressed, those that they had heard that day. The next set of meetings was with the other side. All the clergy became confused. As we drove off in the evening, someone called out to me: 'Archbishop, I know what you are doing. You're messing with our heads.' It was a wise comment, recognizing that contact with people in conflict always affects our perceptions. It is to identify and reflect on the impact of perceptual change that makes supervision necessary.

Many people will be very familiar with some conflict in which they have found themselves caught. Perhaps they know a couple whose marriage is facing a bitter collapse. They meet friends of the wife and are told that the husband has been totally unreasonable for so many reasons. They meet friends of the husband who talks of the way the wife controlled him and spent money so fast. In each conversation what they want to say is, 'but it's more complicated than that!' The friends have simplified things to the point where one side is to blame. The truth is deep and historic, sending out roots in all sorts of directions that are to do with everything from the model the couple inherited from their own upbringings to the way in which they communicated. There will be times when there is some simplicity; for example, violence or emotional abuse where safety demands separation. The aim of reconciliation in such cases may very likely not be restoration of co-habitation but rather the capacity to move on towards personal healing and hope, or in the case of an abuser, to repentance and change.

That being said, and with all due precautions, there are some questions where the answers are very often decisive to the future hopes of any kind of reconciliation. They are very often not questions put directly, because that always invites the answer that the interviewee thinks is wanted. Many interviewees will be glad to talk and want the facilitator to see it their way.

The key ones are about dreams and objectives. Is it possible to sense a war weariness? What would a good outcome look like in their own minds? How deep is the bitterness? Can the other side have any merits? Something that is extremely rare but is also a sign of immense hope is when one hears the view – or the echo of the view – of the other put across, not as something to be agreed with, but with even the smallest level of mutual understanding or empathy.

The great strength of the facilitator is that they need not pretend to knowledge that they do not have. Asking foolish questions is not foolish when you are an outsider. Asking apparently foolish questions is often a way of giving agency and respect to those involved.

In John's Gospel, chapter 5, John tells of Jesus going to the Temple in Jerusalem for a big festival. He visits a pool at Beth-zatha, which was believed to have healing properties when the waters stirred. Many sick people were there, and Jesus approaches one who had lain there all his life: 'When Jesus saw him lying there and knew that he had been there a long time, he said to him, "Do you want to be made well?"' (verse 6, NRSV). The reader's first reaction is often, 'What a daft question!' He had been there for thirty-eight years. Yet it was the opposite of daft. It gave the man choice, provoked self-reflection, and meant that the sign Jesus performed to heal him was done with him, not to him. There is always a question in the back of one's mind: 'What do the participants in this struggle want? Do they want peace?' It is rare that the question is put so bluntly, but as we will see further down the line, there are many ways of getting to the answer and there will have to be a point where the challenge of desire is faced.

DANGERS

As discussed earlier, throughout the process there are dangers, in particular those deriving from *overspeed* and *overreach*. Researching will prepare facilitators to anticipate those dangers, to avoid them or to have plans ready to face them.

Overspeed. In all conflicts that have reached a level of maturity and where there is genuinely a sense that it is necessary to try something new if the struggle is ever to end, there is a desire for speed. Peacemaking tends to have two speeds: stationary and rush. Both are dangerous. The latter is often encouraged by those around, by circumstances and in public situations by the media.

The mystery of peace is not only that for those in conflict it is hard to imagine but also that its coming seems to take either for ever, or far less time than one might fear. In one case, patience is lost and with it progress. In the other, opportunities are often not taken because peace has slipped in by surprise. The Middle East has a long history of overlooked opportunities. By contrast, in one African country a handshake at church between two leaders who could have torn the country apart led a few weeks later to them spending a day together alone, and to the establishment of peace. They had the wisdom to grip the unexpected opportunity, and broke conventional approaches to do it.

In a conversation while I was writing this chapter in the summer of 2021, I was invited to get involved in a relatively large-scale peacebuilding process. I was very doubtful, but the doubts diminished enormously when the person with whom I was talking said, 'Of course, the first stage of design, mapping, planning and research, is going to take a long time.' The sense of that comment showed a great deal of realism.

In Ogoni the research became a very important part of the process and to my surprise did lead to a slight change in the mood – although I am not in any way claiming that I made much difference. The start made at the time I was involved was followed up by more skilled, more local people who achieved much more significant progress. The most effective facilitator was Bishop Matthew Kukah (now Roman Catholic Bishop of Sokoto). Having already played a key role in numerous Nigerian disputes, up to and including national level, he renewed the momentum of the reconciliation work in Ogoni. His book, *Witness to Reconciliation*, to be published in 2022, is a magisterial account of both the stories and the approaches. Fifteen years later the list of those who have been involved is long, but the credit for the small change made goes to the people of Ogoni.

Overreach and *underreach* are two sides of the same coin. An overreach of imagination leads to the illusion that great difficulties can be overcome in the twinkling of an eye and bitterness will evaporate with a touch of sense. Underreach is the problem of looking at the gaps and not the potential bridges. The first is a sign that the lessons of the research are not sinking in with the facilitator and the second that the pain has become overwhelming.

Both happen easily. In the difficult discussions within the Church of England over the question of ordaining women as bishops, the biggest step was to imagine that a way forward could be found. In some of the conversations, several groups were involved. In one of them the facilitator was obviously pushing a solution. It led to all sides digging their heels in. The facilitator was not arrogant or bad at their job, but they were desperate for progress and sought to take things faster than was the mood of the participants.

By contrast, earlier in the process, after a major setback, all and sundry spoke of needing five years at least to chart a way forward that ended taking less than two, owing to the desire by all concerned to find such a way. The setback opened the way to progress.

The third crucial error is leaving out those participants who matter, and its twin, giving any group too much profile and thus a disempowering veto at the wrong moment. Most conflicts have someone or some group that, like Voldemort in Harry Potter, cannot be named. It may be a powerful militia or an important and shadowy government figure. In Ogoni there were constant rumours about who was lifting the oil. There was also clear evidence of criminal gangs who were very willing to threaten violence.

The identification of those who matter is one of great political sensitivity. If a person or group is left out, they will very often seek to become disruptive. On the other hand, including a genuinely marginal figure gives them influence and importance and further complicates the process. Embracing complexity is one thing, adding to it without genuine need is quite another. The arithmetic of the relationships is worth recalling. Two groups and a facilitator mean that the process has three relationships, the parties to each other and each to the facilitator. Go up to three groups and a facilitator and the number of relationships becomes six. Go up to ten and it becomes forty-five.

At this point scale poses its own questions. In a civil conflict everyone seeks to show that they are the most valid representatives of the people. The very act of accepting the claim and giving them a seat at the table means that they acquire far more legitimacy. They also set up their post-conflict trajectory to power. In other words, the stakes are very high indeed. Excluding those with a claim that has validity may drive them to attention-seeking violence.

There are many opt-outs from these types of decisions and many ways round it. The opt-outs are too easily cop-outs.

The researching should give benchmarks for testing the validity of claims to participation. History will show the extent to which they have taken significant risks, mobilized large numbers of people, or in places where elections have some substance, where they have been successful. Research and attentive listening also reveal those who have been marginalized and need to be heard. What is not said, or what is dismissed, is as important as what is said.

Three groups are very often forgotten. First are women. The harsh reality is that whether it is at community level or in war, the significance of women is usually forgotten until too late. They matter for many reasons. They are at least half the population and, as human beings, of equal dignity before God to men, whatever the culture says. They are remarkably vulnerable in armed conflict, especially to sexual abuse. They are the ones who find themselves driven from the homes where they farm, without support, and living in IDP or refugee camps. They bury the dead, whether spouses, children, siblings, friends or parents. It is almost unknown for an effective peace to be made and for a process of peacebuilding to become embedded unless women's groups are centrally involved, and their voice is heard.

Women will perform very central roles in peacebuilding if given the opportunity. In more patriarchal societies, the need to understand what they can do without undue risk is a major task of researching. The spouses of leaders are often given significantly large roles without the training or education required. They will frequently be highly educated but much neglected. Researching should reveal both the most gifted and the requirements in every group for training in building peace.

Second are youths. The definition of youth varies from the western culture, where it will typically mean teenage and early twenties, and in some other places anyone less than forty. Youths are often forgotten, although in most wars they are the main combatants and thus have the most interest in ending or occasionally in continuing the struggle. They may be drawn into fighting as children, with resulting intense trauma. They will have the ability to end the war if they can be brought into a position where they are willing and trained and equipped not to participate.

In community disputes they remain very important as, like women, they will often be done to rather than doing. In families that are in difficulty they will often be the ones longing for settlement and stability, with an equal interest in and love for the disputing parties and no desire to be manipulated into taking sides.

Third are traditional mediators. There is a remarkable arrogance in some outside facilitators that consists in assuming that because there is conflict in a society, it contains nobody with reconciliation skills. Most societies have developed ways of facing conflicting ambitions for power, issues around land ownership and boundaries, conflicts between herders and farmers, neighbour disputes, community breakdown, and marriage and family divisions. They will also very likely have customary law that supports answers. In Rwanda, after the genocide of 1993, local village courts were essential to holding accountable those who had committed crimes and enabling those who had suffered to hear their story. In Burundi there existed a tradition of wise mediators. This group was suppressed in the colonial period lest they become community leaders against the colonial government. Researching must show whether such traditions work or not, so as to go with the grain and not against it.

In many, even most, communities there are equivalents. There may be a church or other religious group that operates as a mediator. There are often individuals who are known as peacemakers.

At the heart of researching is understanding what the weave of the conflict is and of the group and groups in which it is set. Above all, research seeks to enable facilitators to develop confidence in knowing their own ignorance and in being able to know those involved and be known.

Mapping should reveal those who do not seek to participate but prefer to work in the shadows, not in some conspiracy theory imagination but in hidden reality, undermining progress. This has been discussed earlier, and shadow figures and spoilers are among the easiest to miss. Their significance is that their power is real but not evident. Many of those who claim participation in a process will have power that is evident but not real. In armed conflict it is essential to know where the arms and logistics come from, who pays, and how and from where they get the money. In a community it matters if groups are part of an outside network with a wider agenda. In a church where there is a deep divide it is always possible that broader groups are seeking to expand their influence within a denomination.

The danger in looking for shadows and spoilers is that people can become caught up in conspiracy theories. However, even hearing false ideas is useful in the process of research as an indicator of mood. The volume and attraction of conspiracy theory in a group or society is very frequently an early warning of more violent conflict.

KNOWING THAT THE RESEARCH IS BEARING FRUIT

The move from the first to the second R, Relating, should be seamless. Researching goes on throughout the entire journey as all involved need to be able to expect that they will gain a better understanding. So how does the facilitator know that it is time to start spinning the second plate?

The most important sign is that they can tell the story of the conflict from the different perspectives of those involved in the process, in a way that each of them can recognize. Thus, in Ogoni a good sign would have been for Shell to hear the local community tell the story from Shell's point of view in a way recognizable to Shell. More importantly still, given the power of Shell, MOSOP leaders, women, youths and civil society observers who had been helping the Ogoni people should recognize their own view of the conflict when Shell told the story from the local as if from the community's point of view.

Research does not bring solutions; it brings out the next plate, with its deepening relationships.

SUMMARY

- Researching is a long process that continues right through the journey of peacemaking.
- Researching takes the peacebuilder from unconscious to conscious ignorance.
- It should enable mapping of the conflict and recognition of complexity.
- It goes from desktop analysis to interviews and meetings in the field.

- It must include women, youths and traditional peacebuilders, whether in a family or a war.
- It should enable discernment about the roles and categories of different people.
- Supervision matters to avoid being traumatized or misled.
- It will reveal the problems and may reveal ways forward.

POINTS TO PONDER

- If you know of a conflict, how much do you really know? Have you decided that you know everything before you really do? Does that happen if you are caught up in a dispute?
- Look at some quarrel, dispute or conflict you know about. Whose voices are not heard? Who is forgotten?
- Try getting together with someone and exchanging the story of a dispute familiar to you, four times. Twice tell the story from one side, and then twice from the other? Can you do it? (It is not unusual to answer no.) What are the biggest challenges?
- Read John 5. If reading the Bible is not part of your normal life don't try to understand everything but ask some questions. Who are the key people involved? How would you describe the quarrel? How does Jesus treat the man who is healed? Before and after? How does he treat Jesus?

5

Relating – the Power of Love

A young woman – an economic migrant – arrives in a village belonging to an enemy. She is accompanied by her mother-in-law, who had grown up in the village. For the latter it is reverse migration. She had gone to the enemy country, also as an economic migrant perhaps twenty years earlier, with her husband and two sons. The men had died after a few years, leaving two daughters-in-law and no grandchildren. In desperation, one daughter-in-law goes back to her paternal home, and the other joins in the frightening and dangerous process of travel.

It is a love story. The young woman and her mother-in-law love each other. The time is a little over three thousand years ago. The region is what we now call the Holy Lands. The story is that of Ruth, a most beautiful book in the Old Testament. But it could have been today. We have economic migration, refugees, ancient hatred and wars, the travel of desperate people to places they do not know. They support each other on the way; they often die. Occasionally the ending is happy. That is the case in the case of Ruth and Naomi, where Ruth meets a man, they marry and have children.

The story is so much deeper than that, of course. It is a love story where, as in all the best love stories, the main characters cross boundaries, show courage, are imaginative and see solutions that are not visible to anyone else, and in this case everyone is kept and held in the love of God.

That is the link to two of the best-known and most overwhelming of the statements on love in the New Testament. In John's first letter he says baldly, 'God is love.'[1] Earlier on he has made it clear that the letter is a witness and testimony to what he has experienced and seen in meeting Jesus and following him for three years. The second overwhelming statement is in John's Gospel, 'For God so loved the world that he gave his only Son, so that all who believed in him should not perish but have eternal life' (John 3.16, NRSV). These verses speak of the love of God as boundary busting, leaping over the gap between God and human beings. The leap is made by God and it is a leap of reconciling love.

The action of Jesus breaks all boundaries and dissolves the barriers that reinforce those boundaries. In John 3 Jesus is in conversation with a Jewish leader and teacher. In John 4 he engages first with a woman from an enemy people (a Samaritan) and then with the child of a senior official for the king of the region that included Galilee. In John 5 he heals a man on the Sabbath, breaking the barrier of what the leaders interpreted as work, expressed in God's commands not to work on the Sabbath.

That is still the work of God today and the Church is at its glorious best when it seeks to demonstrate the pure and holy love of God in breaking barriers and when with courage it stands with those whose experience is of being barred from leading a full life, what Jesus calls an abundant life.

Because it is the work of God it is also the best way for the world. Reconciliation is not the exclusive possession of the Church or of the religious. Ruth is not from Israel yet God's work of reconciliation is active in her life and character. Peacebuilding and the desire for peace is hardwired into the desire of most people. To make it happen is to act well. To make it happen well requires relationships founded on love, whatever more they also need. The reconciliation that God gives through love is more abundant than we can imagine. It is not just barely sufficient, a sort of just-about-enough love for reducing conflict, but when shared, reconciliation grows and expands and overflows. In John 6 Jesus feeds five thousand with a few loaves and fish, and twelve baskets of food are left over. In this act we see the meeting of physical need, but much more than that the super-abundance of the provision of all that is needed. So it is with reconciliation. It can never run out when it is what we aim for.

As it is presented in the Bible, love is far more than an emotion. It is something of great activity. God does not sit in heaven saying soppily, 'I love people'; God acts, and it is through God's action that we perceive God's love. It was God's love that carried Ruth and her mother-in-law, Naomi, through the agony of bereavement back to Bethlehem, Naomi's home. It was God's love that brought Ruth into contact with Boaz, the landowner and cousin of Naomi. It was God's love that opened Ruth and Boaz's hearts to love for one another and it was God's love that meant that the resulting child was King David's grandfather.

In other words, God's love broke down every barrier in order to ensure that Israel's second – and model – king was partly Moabite, an enemy. The Book of Ruth is many beautiful things, but it is centrally a book about reconciliation.

In doing so it points forward to Jesus, the ultimate, absolute, definitive reconciler, and shows that love is not just what we feel but is true when it is what we do.

The second 'R' is relating, and it is founded on love.

All reconciliation work deals with the bitterest and most powerful of human emotions, emotions very often justified by the terrible circumstances faced. A family quarrel of great bitterness has a capacity to penetrate the hardest emotional armour and hurt deeply. A church that is riven by disagreement has a toxicity that is the opposite of what its members hope for and seek. Community quarrels are hard-edged because the participants are continually with each other or seeing each other. As for violent conflict and struggle – the mixture of terror, pride, hatred and ambition is an emotional cocktail that historically has led to the greatest courage and the greatest cruelty.

The only force that can cross the boundaries is love. The role of the people and groups that facilitate reconciliation is not a functional and mechanical one characterized by technique, but a relational one characterized by love. Of course, love is not all we need (sorry, The Beatles), but any action not based in love and driven by love is, to quote St Paul in 1 Corinthians 13, nothing but a sounding gong or a clanging cymbal. It is noise without substance.

One of the most effective peacebuilders I have met is Canon Andrew White, with whom I worked for almost three years when I was at Coventry Cathedral. He is a controversial figure, larger than life, physically as well as everything else. Having watched him in action, one thing that is overwhelming is his gift for relating to people, because they know he loves them.

It was that love, and the risks he took to see people, that enabled Andrew to play a key role[2] in gathering those who signed the Alexandria Declaration, which sought to undermine the religious blockages in peacemaking. Many of the signatories were bitter enemies; his friendship was a common factor to them all.

For several years he had visited Jerusalem and the other parts of the Holy Lands continually. At times in places of heavy fighting, he had done the research that enabled him to see who needed to be involved. All this time the situation was deteriorating, but that did not cause unreasonable rush. Eventually he had built relationships strong enough to get permission to hold a meeting in Alexandria, supported by the UK Foreign Office, in which the traditional enemies came together to call for peace and commit themselves to work for it. The final, three-day negotiation was chaired superbly by the then Archbishop of Canterbury, Lord Carey of Clifton as he now is.

The impact of the Declaration had the potential to open a door that had been neglected in the Oslo peace process: that of religious leaders. It illustrates the need to get the right people involved.

The Muslims included a Grand Mufti (a very senior judge) as well as a number of sheikhs and imams, religious teachers with a strong political and juridical role. The Jewish figures included an Israeli government minister and rabbis, including from a settlement in the Occupied Territories. They had already been building links across the barriers of conflict, and one of the most important parts of everyone's research was to identify which of the apparently hard-line figures behaved in a way that opened opportunities for peacebuilding.

The meeting exhibited partnership. Apart from the Archbishop of Canterbury, there was involvement by diplomatic groups and other organizations with whom relationships had been built. All were crucial, including the ones who had done invisible preparatory work but got little or no credit in the final outcome.

The research demonstrated what could and could not be done. A declaration was possible but not a peace settlement; the latter would need a more comprehensive process. The necessary time was taken. The signatories were in a place to go on working together.

Working with Andrew demonstrated that he loved genuinely but was also realistic about those he worked with. They were not remotely all 'good people'. A number had been involved with violence. The various regional governments that had some involvement were not all being helpful out of mere goodwill. There was a desire to instrumentalize the process for their own reasons, many of which were more about gaining advantage than making peace.

These behaviours are part of being human and part of the corrosive impact of conflict. It undermines all that is best and most selfless, and draws the mind, morals and emotions into a place where personal power seeking and advantage gaining, by any means, are not just temptations but normal ways of living. It is not a criticism of the Oslo process; the focus in Oslo was on the central, political issues. However, if the old slogan and wisdom of peacebuilding – 'top down, middle out, bottom up – is to be the aim, then the religious actors will need to be involved in most countries in the world. Nowhere is that more important than in Jerusalem, Israel and Palestine. Religious actors will seldom bring the 'top down', but they may ease the way for political leadership, and they tend to be part of networks that go from grassroots to presidential mansions. Moreover, for those whose faith is more than skin deep, loyalty to God and faith will matter more than anything else and is the most powerful possible force for good, or evil.

Relating love-in-action. To return to John's Gospel, the gospel of the holy love of God, the way that Jesus loves, shows the true nature of reconciling love.

All four Gospels tell us that on the night of his betrayal, arrest and trial, Jesus held a Passover meal, a celebration of the liberation of God's people, the Israelites from Egypt under the leadership of Moses. According to John, chapter 13, before the meal he took off his outer clothing, wrapped a towel around himself and washed his disciples' feet, including those of Judas, who he knew was planning to betray him. John says, 'Having loved his own who were in the world, he loved them to the end.'[3] The Greek word for 'end' can be translated in a variety of ways, but has the sense of completely, to the finish, to the limit.

Together with going to be crucified, this is the central demonstration by Jesus of the nature of God's love and of the way he wants human beings to love one another: we are to love to the limit. The Church above all should show this love. The leaders of this world should show this love. I remember a remarkable moment in the concluding service of a gathering of the senior leaders of the Anglican Communion from around the world. At the end of a very difficult meeting, full of conflict, we washed each other's feet. It is more difficult to receive than to do, for it requires one to submit to being loved, to having something done for you by someone who you feel is at least your equal and very often your superior. Yet it is a channel for the healing of relationships when done properly.

The proper response of love is temporarily to suspend judgement but not wisdom. Judgement in this sense, the sense of Jesus' command in the Sermon on the Mount,[4] is a pretence of objective and virtuous distance. The basis of the incarnation, of God taking flesh and being fully human in Jesus, is that identification with human beings is complete. We do not have that ability, but we can be creatively imaginative.

On one occasion, in the Niger Delta I visited a remote town, at that time only accessible by boat through the creeks of the wetlands. There were three of us in the group. When we arrived, we were taken to see a gang leader. He was slightly drunk and very threatening. He declared that we should be killed – a statement that was delivered all in the local language and that he was persuaded not to carry out by our local companion. We were 'invited' to stay overnight in a local guest house.

The next morning, he reappeared and took us on a tour of the town. A couple of miles away was a flow-station, a centre of oil production with the local field producing more than a hundred thousand barrels per day of very high-quality crude. Its generators gave it twenty-four-hour, reliable electricity for the plant and equipment, as well as for air conditioning, light and entertainment. Its helicopters could whisk people in and out and provide easy access to medical facilities. There was clean water and good food.

By contrast the town was a place of tragedy. It sat above the oilfield, a source of enormous wealth but only to others. Sewage ran down the main street, where children played. There was no regular electricity. Food was terrible, clean water absent, education for the next generation non-existent, medical care a mere dream. Malaria was endemic. Violence was constant in order to gain control and seek income from local contractors and others. It was at the very gates of hell.

Our 'host' was not a good man by most standards and was probably very bad indeed in many people's eyes. Yet he had grown up there, comfort and wealth in sight in the near distance, and filth and violence his normal life. To judge would be to say that if I were him, I would have been better. To show wisdom would be to empathize with the sheer misery of his life and prospects but not to collude with the decisions he made.

So perhaps love *is* all we need (spot on, The Beatles): but we need to reimagine love.

Many people know the Apostle Paul's beautiful hymn to love in 1 Corinthians 13. It is often read at weddings, which puts a sweet, fluffy coating of sugar on it. When the words are taken and applied as they are meant, it is a soaring vision of foundations in peace for the world around us.

> If I speak in the tongues of mortals and of angels, but do not have love, I am a noisy gong or a clanging cymbal. [2] And if I have prophetic powers, and understand all mysteries and all knowledge, and if I have all faith, so as to remove mountains, but do not have love, I am nothing. [3] If I give away all my possessions, and if I hand over my body so that I may boast, but do not have love, I gain nothing.
>
> [4] Love is patient; love is kind; love is not envious or boastful or arrogant [5] or rude. It does not insist on

its own way; it is not irritable or resentful; [6] it does not rejoice in wrongdoing, but rejoices in the truth. [7] It bears all things, believes all things, hopes all things, endures all things.

[8] Love never ends. But as for prophecies, they will come to an end; as for tongues, they will cease; as for knowledge, it will come to an end. [9] For we know only in part, and we prophesy only in part; [10] but when the complete comes, the partial will come to an end. [11] When I was a child, I spoke like a child, I thought like a child, I reasoned like a child; when I became an adult, I put an end to childish ways. [12] For now we see in a mirror, dimly, but then we will see face to face. Now I know only in part; then I will know fully, even as I have been fully known. [13] And now faith, hope, and love abide, these three; and the greatest of these is love. (1 Cor. 13, NRSV)

PATIENCE

Peacebuilding requires patience in love. The nature of conflict is to generate suspicion. Facing suspicion and the irrationality that comes with it requires a deep love and understanding in facilitators as they seek to untangle the belief that they are taking sides. Part of the suspicion will be born out of years of being tricked and deceived. At the Congress of Vienna in 1815, ending the Revolutionary and Napoleonic Wars, it is reported anecdotally that when the Chancellor of the Austro-Hungarian Empire heard that the leading French representative, Talleyrand, had died (he had not, in fact), he said, 'Now what does he mean by that?' Talleyrand was notorious for changing sides, and for his duplicity. Conflict involves deception, and deception breeds suspicion.

Patience is seen by time given. It is represented by long-term commitment. More than that, the commitment must be organizational, not just individual. There is something deeply addictive about being seen to be indispensable, but it is only of any benefit to the person concerned, never to the cause they support. Too often in facilitating peacebuilding there is dependence on a star figure. The more of a star they are the less they are able to give time and patience to one place.

The Alexandria Declaration depended to some degree on the skill of Canon Andrew White. When he became caught up in other equally important areas momentum failed. Relationships need nurturing. No individual can manage the commitment and be sure to be available as much as required. However, it is possible to create institutional links where trust is created over time by a consistent and patient commitment through a group.

The nature of institutions is, however, bureaucratic. A clear example is the United Nations Organization. Created in 1945 it has grown into a vast network of specialist groups within the UN family. At its centre sits the Security Council (UNSC), served by the Secretary General. Almost all who work in it know and see its faults and the inertia that develops because of the rivalries among the P5, the Permanent Five members of the UNSC, who are able to veto or otherwise block UN activities in peacebuilding.

It is easy to criticize, and there is plenty of valid criticism, but nobody has come up with anything better. The UN has built up great skill in intervening in conflicts and has both an unrivalled view of what is happening in confrontations around the world and wisdom in how to approach them. The agendas of its members may frustrate it plans, but that is not its fault. Most of all, it avoids the star system.

The single hero figure and the UN represent the two ends of a process of peacebuilding. One end struggles with patience and resilient long-term commitment and thus initiatives run out of steam. The other is prone to being unable to act in time while its members work out their interests. The first can build good relationships with an individual. The second has the methods but misses the personal approach.

Peacebuilding and reconciliation facilitation includes the necessity to hold the two together. Earlier on in this chapter we looked at John 13 and the account of Jesus washing the feet of his disciples. He had been committed to them for three years or so, and the moment was approaching when he would go, and they would remain. Their capacity to take over and to live as they were called to by him was essential to the whole of God's plan for the world. As in so much in the Bible, God's love is shown in patience and in partnership with human beings.

Jesus has built a community and in the washing of the feet was setting a pattern for its life. It is an act that ensures that the community is people- rather than task-focused, and this is achieved through obeying his command to 'love one another as I have loved you'.

Those who are going to be involved in facilitating reconciliation must therefore be committed to working in a team, with no stars among them and a long-term vision in which their contribution may well never be recognized. They will need love that patiently suffers setbacks and yet continues, perhaps from a different approach. They will need to see those involved in the conflict not as resources to be managed and manipulated but as human beings to be liberated from the struggles in which they find themselves.

Loving and Keeping Distance

Where are the limits in love? At what point does wisdom say, 'Do not meet such and such a person'?

In the 1950s a Dutch Christian, using the name Brother Andrew, began to reach out to Christians behind what was called the Iron Curtain.[5] He carried out this work for many years,[6] but after he had stepped back he continued to visit terrorist groups in order to build relationships with their leaders and to speak to them of peace. He did all this without publicity, public funding or self-advertisement. Its impact cannot be measured yet the risks were very considerable.

First was the risk meeting the people he did. Second was the risk to his reputation. To meet people who are known to be involved in violence, or in a domestic situation, in abuse of one kind or another, is often seen as collusion. It risks being shut out from speaking to those on the other side on the grounds that if you have met the bad person you must be their friend, and my enemy's friend is my enemy. Third, it risks losing the wisdom of seeing the reality of those you deal with (as discussed above in Chapter 2). One terrorist I met was in appearance and manner a sort of Father Christmas. He was small and round, smiled the whole time and told jokes. He also killed a lot of people, but his charm somehow seemed to overshadow the evil. Another, a former Head of State, spent an hour explaining that the rumours of the number of people he had killed were very exaggerated. So charismatic was he that I caught myself thinking, 'Well, that's not too bad.' It was only later that reality sank in more clearly when I compared notes with others.

Evil is attractive in a horrible way. The villains in novels and plays are often more interesting than the heroes. Look at Satan in Milton's *Paradise Lost*, or at Shakespeare's *Richard III*, *Macbeth* or *Coriolanus*. Fiction reflects reality. Where then are the limits and how does a facilitator avoid being sucked into collusion?

Love should not be blind. Researching will have demonstrated the character and history of the main parties to a conflict. To emphasize what has been said already, humility in the facilitator, when with colleagues or a supervisor, will enable them to be aware what their motivations are. Some participants in a conflict are deeply committed to power seeking and active hatred. Recognizing who those are will seldom be the role only of one person.

There are some obvious rules. If there is a family where the breakup of a marriage is linked to abuse of children, or to substance abuse that is not admitted, or to violence where there is an attempt at self-justification, then reconciliation will almost always mean seeking to find the least damaging parting possible.

The same may well be the case with regard to racist activity or other systematic and calculated oppression of minorities or the vulnerable. One test as to limits is the possibility of one party being willing to repent and make reparations. This was the test imposed by the South African Truth and Reconciliation Commission.[7] Those who participated in acknowledging their crimes could hope to share in the amnesty only if they were willing to be honest (Truth) in front of victims and to demonstrate that they understood what they had done wrong.

Talal Asad,[8] in a very powerful examination of the sociology of suicide bombing, saw this most extreme and irreconcilable of violent acts as requiring a violent response from law enforcement that says 'some humans have to be treated violently in order that humanity can be redeemed'. Love is not infallible but must be held in a moral framework so that 'being loving' cannot become an excuse for behaving wrongly or ignoring injustice. Temporarily suspending judgement must not become the toleration of injustice. Love wrongly expressed may lead to great evil and require violence to be faced. There are some people who, in police terms, need to be removed from a conflict if there is to be hope of reconciliation. That removal is a demonstration of a love for the majority whom they may influence by fear or favour. To bring them into reconciliation the worst of the spoilers may have to be faced and not included in the process.

SUMMARY

- Love is of the very nature of God, and it is in love for human beings that God opens the way to reconciliation with God and also with each other.
- Reconciliation is a fruit of abundant love and is itself abundant.
- Relationships of love-in-action are the foundation of reconciliation. The love must be genuine.
- However, love-in-action is characterized by the words used by Paul in 1 Corinthians 13, above all patience. Reconciliation takes time.

- Love in reconciliation will often need to suspend judgement, but never to lose wisdom. It must discern where evil lies in individuals and structures and avoid being drawn into collusive and co-dependent behaviour.

POINTS TO PONDER

- Think of the best examples you know of love-in-action. It may be family, or community, or more widely. What are its characteristics, compare them with 1 Corinthians 13.
- How do you avoid being taken in by charming villains or fascinating structures of evil? What would be examples you have seen, perhaps just in one person, or in history?
- Where have you seen the best examples of care that are emotionally committed but still wise and discerning?

Exercise

Your local primary school, St Thomas, in the Diocese of Barchester, is on the edge of town, between a series of small villages and an outer estate. It is a Church of England school, where the vicar chairs the school governors. The estate has high unemployment and considerable deprivation, made worse by the closure of a local shoe factory about three years ago. The local church, St Thomas the Pompous (a lesser-known Barchester saint of the sixth century), has a very strong tradition of involvement with the community. It runs a food bank in partnership with other churches and a mosque, has a debt-counselling centre and a job club. It also is part of a group with churches in all four of the local villages, which are traditional country settings, with strong communities and ancient buildings. The town church was built in the 1960s.

Two major social changes are going on. First, a large number of asylum seekers are being sent to the estate and housed there. The town has one part with a significant, mainly South Indian population. Community relationships have been very good. However, the asylum seekers are from numerous other places, especially Syria, parts of Africa caught in war, and Afghanistan. School places for unaccompanied children are stretching the facilities of the school, food bank, social care and local doctors' practice. Funding cuts have meant the council is very short of money. Waiting lists for housing are growing, affecting the children of people on the estate. There is ethnic tension that has shown itself in the church feeling less welcoming and some comments that 'they should go somewhere else'.

In order to raise money, the council is selling some land it owns between the town and the nearest village. It is doing this in partnership with the Diocese of Barchester, which also owns land in the same area. The bigger development is attracting a lot of bids from developers to build executive housing for commuters at a new railway station connecting to Barchester itself, a financial services hub.

The vicar is caught. Interfaith relations are beginning to struggle. The villages are up in arms at being 'joined' to the town by the new housing. The school has gone down an OFSTED (quality assessment) grade, which is felt by the staff to be very unfair considering the pressure they are under. The vicar and her colleagues want to see the village churches rise to the new challenge. The churches are very keen not to.

The staff team have asked you, as the Diocesan Reconciler, to help.

Can you start by mapping a little of the various conflicts? In a group of three or so, look at the research you want to do, and invent the answers (keep it relatively short!). Second, who do you need to build relationships with? How will you overcome the problem that you are from the diocese that is contributing to the issues?

Warning: this story is going to extend through Part II. Feel free to adjust the jargon for a non-Anglican situation or reimagine the case in terms of your own circumstances, but with the similar challenge of large-scale change in a conservative area with a religious institution that seeks to serve the population.

6

Relieving Need – Love Made Visible

The Democratic Republic of the Congo is enormous. To fly from one side to the other is a journey of around 2,000 kilometres (1,400 miles). Much of it is forest. Its historic main highway is the river. Transport other than by river or air is very difficult indeed.

Its history over the last 150 years is terrible. It was for decades the personal property of the King of Belgium, whose colonial rule was appalling even by contemporary standards and a source of scandal before the First World War. Joseph Conrad wrote a book about a river trip called *Heart of Darkness* (turned into a film set in Vietnam and Cambodia by Francis Ford Coppola, *Apocalypse Now*). The DRC was then a Belgian colony, again badly run until it was given unprepared independence in 1960.

Civil war and strife combined with corrupt and tyrannical government have been two of many plagues in the DRC much of the time ever since. Since the mid-1990s more than four million people have died directly and indirectly from war. In the east there have been severe outbreaks of Ebola, measles is rife, as are most tropical diseases. More than 130 militia groups operate under warlords.

Goma is a city on the Rwandan border, set amid remarkable beauty, like much of the country. Lake Bukavu is on one side. Mount Nyiragongo, a very active volcano, on another. The city is often shaken by earthquakes or threatened and damaged by huge flows of lava. The lake contains vast quantities of methane in solution, which might escape, covering the city. In surrounding forests there is a national park with gorillas.

My friend Désiré Mukanirwa was an Anglican parish priest when I first met him in 2005, at a conference in Geneva. He was training in international development. In 2009 I visited him in Goma, in his parish. The city was under siege and many of the NGOs had been forced to go home. We spent time training people in reconciliation at a local level. He took me to a refugee camp, one of a number with a total of about a quarter of a million people in the region. Appalled, I asked him, 'But what can you do?' 'We do what God enables us to' was his calm reply. His church building, damaged in an earthquake and nearly destroyed by a lava flow, was rickety but full of people. His home was full of women, most of whom had been raped in the conflicts, expelled from their communities and now receiving medical help, pastoral care and food from Désiré, and his wife Claudeline, who taught them a trade in clothes making.

I kept going back, introducing him at the UN, also to a UK government minister leading on international aid. His goodness, cheerfulness and faith caught everyone's imagination. About four years ago he became the first Anglican bishop of Goma. Unchanged by all this, he worked everywhere, travelling into conflict zones where militias threatened to kill him. He organized football competitions, bringing together teams of young men from opposing groups, vulnerable to being recruited as soldiers for the militias. In the morning they played football, then they were fed, and in the afternoon he taught them peacebuilding. The girls were taught and trained by Claudeline.

I last saw him in October 2019, when I spent time at some Ebola centres, in towns in the midst of the conflict, with other remarkable bishops and faith leaders. At the same time another English bishop, Michael Beasley, a skilled epidemiologist, taught a three-day course in Goma to local church leaders, 'Faith in a Time of Ebola', translated into Swahili and French. In the summer of 2020, Désiré died of COVID, after yet another trip into the forests. His funeral was attended by many; he was mourned by most of Goma.

I have told his story and its context at some length because it is a shining example of the holistic nature of peacebuilding, and of reconciliation. Désiré was remarkable, but not exceptional, among effective peacebuilders. His reconciliation work was aimed at relieving needs, all needs, in partnership with numerous NGOs – some, like Tearfund, faith based.

Relieving need is the third R of the six. It is what makes relationships solid. For most of us friendship means something tangible. We talk with friends, enjoy their company, share thoughts and opinions, play sports. But we also turn to them when we find ourselves in trouble. We visit them in hospital, offer them hospitality when they in turn face trouble, even go and see them in prison. The love expressed in true friendship is holistic; it relieves need.

In almost every society on earth, weddings are great occasions for friends and family. The way people get married varies, but it is a rare society where there is not a party of some kind. In many parts of the world the food is special, and very often there is wine or something equivalent. Certainly in the ancient Middle East, weddings were major community affairs. In John's Gospel, chapter 2, Jesus attends a wedding in Galilee, along with his disciples. The wine runs out, his mother prompts him, and Jesus turns the water set aside for rites of purification into wine. Only those serving the wine – Jesus, his mother and the disciples – know about the miracle.

Jesus prevents the public shaming that would go with inadequate supplies of wine. The village would remember such a failure for years. The wine is very good quality. The sign is revealing Jesus as the one who brings radical difference, transforming the water of the Old Testament law into the wine of the Spirit. There is much that can be said, but one obvious point is that there is a huge amount of wine. On a rough calculation it is not far short of two thousand standard bottles. John is not just having fun in telling this, nor is he simply making the point that Jesus was a great guest who really would be welcome at a 'bring a bottle' party. The central points are overwhelming abundance and decisive change.

God's love is expressed in super-abundance. Everything God does is more than just the barely essential. The creation itself is almost literally infinitely wonderful, complicated and beautiful. The love that is the offer of God covers every part of our needs, including the 'luxury' of abundant pleasure in one another and in the great events of life. The purpose of the work of Jesus, in his own words in John 10.10, is that human beings may have *life* in all its abundance.

That abundance is made available through God choosing to work with human beings as partners in prayer and in the actions of demonstrating the love of God. That is the most essential partnership. It is to work with God, to cooperate with God's love in order to be God's hands and eyes, and ears and feet and heart. That is the pattern of Jesus, who says that he only does what he sees the Father doing (John 5.19). Without that partnership with God the church is an NGO with some old buildings. With that partnership it is the channel of God's love.

We know that God is love because God acts in practically loving ways. God's action with and for human beings is normally, although not invariably, through the agency of human beings. The Church is called to be God's image in its partnership with God, love for one another, in learning to forgive and to be a global community of immense diversity united in faith by Christ and living out abundant life in the power of the Holy Spirit of the Creator God.

God's abundance and partnership reaches far beyond the Church. We see love expressed and blessing for human beings through all sorts of agencies, who act in God's ways without being aware of it. The sharing of support through official aid, the innumerable charities in every field of life that work around the world in the places of greatest need, the free gifts given at times of crisis: all these are part of abundant life. Abundant life is declared in John 10.10 by Jesus as the reason for his coming into the world, The finding of abundance is at the heart of God's purpose in reconciling humans to God and, by extension, to one another. It is not enough merely to stop fighting and quarrelling. Abundant life is seen as a vast diversity of character and nature and custom, a diversity that is negotiated in our world through the expression of love and a constant sense of curiosity about others, compassion for them in need, and attention to every need they have.

As has already been seen, Jesus breaks boundaries. In his time the barriers between Jew and non-Jew (the Gentiles) were immense. On one occasion recounted in Mark's Gospel, chapter 7, he was away in a Gentile area, probably to get some time in peace with his disciples. A Syrophoenician woman comes to see him, begging him to help her daughter who is possessed by a demon. Jesus refuses, saying that the 'bread' – of his ministry – is for the family (the Jews), not for the dogs (the Gentiles). She responds with a spirited and deeply biblical riposte, saying that dogs eat what falls from the table, that God's loving mercy is for all the world. In the Old Testament the Gentiles received abundant blessing out of God's abundance towards the people of Israel. Jesus sees the woman's faith and her recognition of him and heals her daughter. He has broken the boundary, acting not on the basis of merit but in an abundant overflowing of God's love expressed in action.

Love Means Love-in-action

Throughout the Christian Bible, and in Jewish understanding of what Christians call the Old Testament, God's love means the knowledge of love through God's action. There is no such thing as passive love, because love expresses itself in action. A friend of mine has worked in hospital chaplaincy in the Midlands for many years. Recently the NHS has agreed to develop the outreach work he has led into a new area of work called 'Compassionate Community Development Across Coventry & Warwickshire'. It's one of those excellent titles that says what it does (as opposed to the Archbishop of Canterbury, he might reply). Compassionate means suffering with and bringing support for people, alongside them, rather than doing things to them. The department recognizes that healthcare includes spiritual care but that the whole human being must be reached. It is an expression of the love of God, from within the NHS, and with the far-reaching aim of bringing abundant life. It is 'love-in-action'.

God's love means action. God is not seen in the Bible as sitting on a remote cloud feeling loving and generally benevolent. The Bible tells of God's love and faithfulness through the experience of people who encounter God directly and indirectly, from Moses as an exiled Israelite and Egyptian leader, meeting God in dramatic miracles, to Esther, caught up in political machinations and finding courage and faith amid God's absence, to Ruth the refugee and throughout the New Testament, especially and supremely in Jesus. Yet even Jesus lived 90 per cent of his life in normal obscurity, with a trade. God's love is not found only in great miracles, but in a day-to-day living presence expressed through the Church and through actions of people in the world. We know God loves us because we experience care and compassion in the world.

LOVE TO THE LIMIT OF CAPACITY

Again though, we have to ask about limits. Bishop Désiré in Goma was at peace with himself and with God because he did what he could, what God enabled him to do, and trusted God for the rest. At its peak the number of refugees in the area he covered went over one million. Yet he still cared and served as much as he could.

Love given and received is an expression of our sharing in the needs of others. In this chapter and before, there has been much talk of partnership, with God and with others. Part of the third R of relieving is that it calls us to *reconciliation in the form of partnership* with others who are seeking to relieve need, and to humility in seeking for each partner to do what they do best.

The absence of such partnership has been a serious problem in many disaster relief operations, although there have been significant improvements in recent decades. A major influence in the work of the armed forces of the UK has been a brilliant book by General Sir Rupert Smith, published in 2006, *The Utility of Force*. Smith starts with the challenge that force continually fails to bring peace or reconciliation in areas of conflict. His argument leads him to the conclusion that peacebuilding, of which he had much experience as a commander of NATO forces in the Balkans, requires extensive partnerships and a team approach, drawing in civil society groups and NGOs. It is a process of partnership.

The obstacles that are usually encountered are in the unwillingness of many institutions to work in partnerships unless they are top of the pack. Peacebuilding requires attitudes of humble collaboration in which every partner seeks to contribute what they can.

The eastern part of the DRC has been a good example, especially during the Ebola crisis, where many of the lessons of the earlier outbreak in West Africa were shared and acted on. In the Ebola treatment centres various NGOs and local health officials worked well under the leadership of the Congolese government and the result was that despite the immense insecurity of the area the outbreak was brought under control.

However, the same collaboration was not seen on the battlefield, where there were poor relationships between regular army and UN forces, and the integration of local groups on wider health and security problems was not pursued. The result is that the disorder and often severe violence has continued.

The same lessons apply closer to home, in normal circumstances of community difficulties. One issue I worked on for a short while in a very diverse UK city involved rising violence between two gangs within the same, recently arrived ethnic group. Working with a – much more knowledgeable – local community leader we interviewed a significant number of people seeking to build up a picture of the problem and to map the conflict. The next stage was for local leaders to form relationships at street level with those from that ethnic group. However, the gangs were also involved in predictable sorts of crime, such as protection, exploitation of sex workers through people trafficking, and low-level but disturbing violence. One part of the response required police action in order to remove the key offenders from the scene. They would otherwise be spoilers and were shadow influences on the more local difficulties. There were also needs for education and job-finding skills, learning English as a second language and work with families. It can easily be seen that such a fairly basic problem would require expertise from those who worked with refugees and asylum seekers, including on legal matters of settlement, schools, education support for adults, jobcentres, debt planning, as well as police and local faith-based groups who could increase the sense of security in a deeply unfamiliar environment for those involved.

Finally, partnership with skilled community mediators was essential in order to create a capacity for working together and giving people the tools to take control of their own destinies through access to other agencies.

Writing it this way makes it all sound very obvious. However, these ingredients were mixed in with funding uncertainty, people who were very busy, varying priorities, and individuals moving from one place to another for work reasons. Continuity of relationship, sharing of knowledge and lack of resource were barriers to effective action. Bringing together such a varied group, who all had their own problems elsewhere, can be close to impossible. For that to happen community leadership is essential from within, and thus the cement that will be necessary to hold the bricks together is likely to be found with those in the community, locally, not from outside.

The need for partnership means that every agency and person does only what they can, but the combination is effective. Yet the difficulty of pulling together disparate teams leads to spending all the time in meetings about how to work together and combine better, rather than on the ground working together and combining well. That can often cause busy people to give up and either work less effectively on their own or simply not participate. It is an opportunity for perfection to be the worst enemy of action. The motto must always be, 'Do what you can, not what you can't.' What you can do may leave huge and glaring gaps, but it is better to try something than to do nothing.

LOVE IS SIMPLE TO EXPRESS, COMPLICATED TO ARRANGE

As has been seen in Chapter 4 on researching, we must accept and embrace the complexity of the problems discovered. At the same time, it is essential to keep the answers focused and as simple as they can be. Partnerships exponentially increase the number of relationships required to be maintained. Not only does the complexity of a conflict increase with more parties involved, but so does the complexity of the response. When the complexity of the response begins to be as great as that of the conflict, the result will be a sharp reduction on what we can do, and a very large increase in what we cannot do.

The essence of simple structures is trust. Mistrust leads to complicating oversight dramatically. Meetings end up much larger because every partner needs to be at everything. Often to show that they are needed every partner will feel a need to give a report. One arrives quickly at that point in a meeting where everything has been said, but not everything has been said by everyone.

Trust without accountability is gambling. There is always a need for a route by which people can express concerns about standards or behaviour, especially where large numbers of volunteers are involved. For facilitators who are at best consciously ignorant, the fear will be that the process of reconciliation is being used to bring advantage. Some of that will be inevitable, and missing it happening is part of the 'only doing what you can' principle. At the same time, keeping the initial two plates, 'Researching' and 'Relating', spinning securely will not only reduce the level of ignorance but also provide good bases for feedback about one's own failures and about manipulation.

IDENTIFYING THE NEEDS

It might seem that this particular 'R' does not always apply. However, it always matters. It may be better camouflaged in places of high resources but the need will still be great. It is just that its shape changes.

At one point I worked with a church in the middle of a university area.[1] The minister (church leader) had been in post for about four years, was very different from his predecessor, and had changed a number of things at the church, including the form of the morning service. Relationships had deteriorated within the church, to the point where it seemed about to split and damage its ministry severely in the process.

Two of us worked together meeting lay and ordained members of the church individually, researching, and spending time getting to know people a little (relating). My instinct was that in this wealthy and very highly educated community of faith, with a strong tradition of large congregations, we could mentally skip the third 'R'. What could a place like that need in terms of physical support?

Thankfully, my colleague was more sensible than I was. Several issues began to surface as we got to know people better. Being curious and being present, listening hard and attentively, began to bring out some common themes.

One was isolation and loneliness. The church abounded with activity, but it was all about doing things. There was little opportunity for its members to form close friendships that would weather the normal storms of life and strengthen them in hard moments. Many families had moved into the area for work and for the very good schools, and found themselves financially very stretched, with consequent strains on their marriages and households. Drugs were easily obtainable and the church youth group for teenagers did not seem to the families to address the issue.

The presenting issue was that the minister had changed the services to make them more student-friendly, seeing the call of that church as being towards the university. He spent a great deal of time on this sort of work. As a result, as one person put it, 'those of us who have been around for a long time feel that we are only valued for what we give'.

Listening to the other group (for the sake of keeping it short I am somewhat simplifying) the story was very different. The minister had felt bullied from the day he arrived, with both he and his family not being welcomed into people's homes, something they were used to at their previous post, where they had been for a long time. It seemed obvious to the generally younger part of the church that the students needed to hear the good news of Jesus Christ, and that the people in the church already were prone to be an obstacle to what they felt was God's call. The list went on and on, and the regional head of that denomination was at her wit's end, worrying about the health of the minister and the future of one of the flagship churches.

Even in such a well-resourced church there were needs for help, physical demonstrations of love. One example was to bring in experts in debt counselling. Another was to encourage home groups to have time to eat together and pray for each other, as well as reading the Bible.

On the other side there was a need for welcome to be symbolized, done in this case through a visiting programme and bring-and-share suppers in groups of twenty, with a town-hall-style question-and-answer session with members of the Eldership group and the minister.

The minister was given access to coaching and further training on leadership, and there was a service of repentance and recommitment, based on the beautiful Methodist Covenant service.

Resources used were thus psychological, time, hospitality, counselling in areas of pressure, and an open acknowledgement of where things had gone wrong.

Everyone has needs, even if they are intangible. Peacebuilding demonstrates love in paying attention to needs. The facilitator may not be able to do everything – in the church example, neither I nor my colleague were anywhere near doing so. But we did what we could, and sought to liberate the resources of the church to make their own reconciliation work.

SUMMARY

- The nature of God's provision is abundance, with generosity to a lavish extent. In the ministry of Jesus, especially in the 'signs'[2] in John's Gospel, abundance often plays a role, particularly in the miracle of the water into wine and the feeding miracles. The abundance is gracious; it is not earned but is a gift of love. Imitating Christ, consciously or not, points us towards relieving need with abundant generosity.
- The actions of meeting need by Jesus are usually in dialogue with the person concerned or with those who can speak for the person concerned, for example Mary and Martha in John 11 when Lazarus is raised from the dead. In this way people are given respect; not treated as objects on

which to demonstrate magic tricks but rather as people of value.

- Love is demonstrated by action. For those caught up in the insecurities of conflict, at any level, proof of love matters and is found through action.
- Relief is not to be guilt inducing. We do what we can, not what we can't. That will, however, be sacrificial and costly.
- Meeting needs with relief will drive us to partnership, and that is always a test of character and values. Are we willing to wash feet, to be obscure and in the background, and see someone else get the credit if that means real progress can be made?
- The central partnership is with God, sometimes unconsciously.
- However complicated the conflict, seek to build trust in the partnership supporting and facilitating and thus to keep that group simple, but enable accountability. Very often the first reconciliation will be among the facilitators and other partners.
- Everyone has needs that will need relieving. In all situations, always. If we can't see them it's because we are not paying attention enough, not researching and relating properly (I speak from foolish experience) – not because they don't exist.

Points to Ponder

- Look closely at one or more of Jesus' miracles, for example the Marriage Feast at Cana in John 2, or

the healing of Bartimaeus in Mark 10.46ff. There
will be surprises but see how agency and dignity
are maintained and abundance and generosity
is demonstrated.
- Try and think honestly and write down how you
feel about working hard and sacrificially and
not getting the credit. In a situation you know,
would you be attracted to help in peacebuilding
on those terms?
- Thinking of a dispute/conflict with which you
are familiar, in a club, church, at work, in the
community or more widely, what are the needs
on every side that require relieving to enable
people to be freer, to have more of life in all
its fullness?
- Regarding the same issue you just thought of,
what can you do, and what can't you do? If you
are someone who prays, write it down and make
a promise to God to do what you can and not
feel guilty about the rest?
- If you worked with someone else, could you do
more? Who might they be?

Case Study (continued)

Go back to the case study at the end of the previous
chapter. Looking at the situation, what are the needs
that require relieving that you, as the facilitator, can
identify? What kind of groups need to be involved?
Who is likely to want to lead? Who do you need to get
onside first?

7

Risking

Judgement is a word that has all sorts of uncomfortable connotations. One of them is that it involves risk. God's judgement is risk free because God is truth, but human judgement is all too fallible.

Even the idea of judgement involves division. It may be the ultimate division at the end of time, or it may simply mean that we have a choice, with different risks in each way forward.

Every journey of peacebuilding and reconciliation has innumerable judgements and choices. It does not matter whether it is at the family level or in war, there will be moments where a choice lies ahead. It will usually include whether to continue or whether to try for a settlement. In the film *Darkest Hour*, set in May 1940, Winston Churchill struggles to keep the British War Cabinet committed to continue the war even after the defeat of France and the triumph of German armies across Europe. One of the lines he is given is: 'You do not negotiate with a tiger when your head is in its mouth.' The Foreign Secretary, Lord Halifax, was arguing that the possibilities of a negotiated peace on poor terms were better than the prospect of complete defeat.

Both arguments convinced some people. Churchill was generally seen to have been right, but even he had grave doubts. The road forked and neither potential route had many attractions; there was no risk-free option.

The role of the facilitator in reconciliation and peacebuilding has been seen to start with Research, to continue while adding the building of deep and resilient Relationships, and third, to add to the first two, commitment to Relieving need, good in itself and a sign of the genuineness of the love in the relationship.

The first three steps are usually the easiest. By the third there are three plates spinning and there is probably a group of partners in peacebuilding, formal or informal, small or large, depending on the level and scale of the dispute. Much research and learning has had the effect of moving from conscious ignorance to partial knowledge. As time progresses, the need for the moral imagination grows and grows and the role of the facilitators becomes increasingly to enable the participants in the quarrel to reimagine their choices. In other words, they must see that there are numerous possible forks in the road and have the will to take the ones leading to peace.

This is a moment when the issues of risk become more and more evident. There is nothing new about the idea. Jesus spoke of it in one of his best-known parables, that of the Two Sons, often called the Parable of the Prodigal Son.[1]

[11] Then Jesus said, 'There was a man who had two sons. [12] The younger of them said to his father, "Father, give me the share of the property that will belong to me." So he divided his property between them. [13] A few days later the younger son gathered all he had and travelled to a distant country, and there he squandered

his property in dissolute living. [14] When he had spent everything, a severe famine took place throughout that country, and he began to be in need. [15] So he went and hired himself out to one of the citizens of that country, who sent him to his fields to feed the pigs. [16] He would gladly have filled himself with the pods that the pigs were eating; and no one gave him anything. [17] But when he came to himself he said, "How many of my father's hired hands have bread enough and to spare, but here I am dying of hunger! [18] I will get up and go to my father, and I will say to him, 'Father, I have sinned against heaven and before you; [19] I am no longer worthy to be called your son; treat me like one of your hired hands.'" [20] So he set off and went to his father. But while he was still far off, his father saw him and was filled with compassion; he ran and put his arms around him and kissed him. [21] Then the son said to him, "Father, I have sinned against heaven and before you; I am no longer worthy to be called your son." [22] But the father said to his slaves, "Quickly, bring out a robe – the best one – and put it on him; put a ring on his finger and sandals on his feet. [23] And get the fatted calf and kill it, and let us eat and celebrate; [24] for this son of mine was dead and is alive again; he was lost and is found!" And they began to celebrate.

[25] 'Now his elder son was in the field; and when he came and approached the house, he heard music and dancing. [26] He called one of the slaves and asked what was going on. [27] He replied, "Your brother has come, and your father has killed the fatted calf, because he has got him back safe and sound." [28] Then he became angry and refused to go in. His father came out and began to plead with him. [29] But he answered his father, "Listen!

For all these years I have been working like a slave for
you, and I have never disobeyed your command; yet
you have never given me even a young goat so that I
might celebrate with my friends. [30] But when this son of
yours came back, who has devoured your property with
prostitutes, you killed the fatted calf for him!" [31] Then
the father said to him, "Son, you are always with me,
and all that is mine is yours. [32] But we had to celebrate
and rejoice, because this brother of yours was dead and
has come to life; he was lost and has been found.'"

The story speaks for itself. The context is that Jesus was
being accused by the religious leaders of mixing with bad
people. In response he tells three stories, of which this is
the longest. In each of them there is a process of something
very valuable being lost, and of the key figure (here, the
father) seeking the thing that is lost. As in all the parables,
it is a story that will have had his listeners oohing and
aahing, taking one side or the other, laughing in places,
shocked in others, but having a sting in the tale. The sting
is that God is like the one who seeks; God reaches out to
the lost, even the lost who are wicked.

You may like to read the story again, see what strikes
you and what surprises you. It is worth noting that we
do not know the conclusion at all. The younger son has
come back, but does he stay? He is not getting the slight
independence of being a hired servant living in the village,
able to get a job elsewhere; he is bound to the family as
a member of it, indebted to his father's forgiving love.
That may be very uncomfortable. The elder son is left
making up his mind as to whether to go into the feast or
not. Will he accept his proper role and restore his brother
completely, or will he stay outside?

As with all of Jesus' stories there are an almost infinite number of ways to read it. In this case, taking the story as one of reconciliation and peacebuilding, I am going to analyse the risks being taken as a trigger to stimulate a sense not only of risk, but also of possibility.

Risks in most journeys of reconciliation can often simply be divided into two main categories, each with a number of sub-categories.

Risk for the Facilitators

The first is the risk for the facilitators. Any kind of reconciliation, especially mediation, brings the risk of much psychological and emotional pain and occasionally the risk of physical harm.

The latter is more dramatic but unusual. Canon Andrew White, of whom I have already written, was present at the siege of the Church of the Nativity in Bethlehem in 2002. The church had been seized by an armed group, with up to two hundred monks and priests in the building. The siege lasted thirty-nine days and was resolved by negotiation. Canon White was present for the vast majority of that time, supporting the negotiations. There was occasional shooting and much confusion, during which time he was under fire.

Subsequently, while working in Baghdad, he was attacked and frequently threatened.

Andrew is something of an exception, as anyone who works with him will tell you, and his experience is certainly more remarkable than that of most facilitators except for people like Terry Waite.

However, one risk affects all those who stand in the middle, which is the pain of being mistrusted, abused and insulted and even hated by all those involved in the conflict. While working in the Niger Delta I was accused of being in the pay of Shell, of the State Government and of the Federal Government by one group. The other group said that I had taken the side of the militia groups. One of my predecessors at Coventry Cathedral, Canon Paul Oestreicher, was at one point accused of being a CIA agent by the intelligence services of the German Democratic Republic (better known as East Germany, the very undemocratic satellite of the USSR in the Cold War) and of being an agent of the Stasi, the intelligence service of East Germany, by the CIA. He joked about it, but it was painful.

In the Parable of the Sons, we see the risks being taken by the father.

The first is that he continues to hope and to look, risking disappointment and public shame (in a strongly honour-/shame-driven culture). He had been terribly ill-treated by his younger son, who in asking for his inheritance has effectively said, 'Dad, I wish you were dead.' Then and now it was an act that would have become the talk of the community and diminished the father in the sight of neighbours. Even though he is evidently rich and respectable, with servants and lands, he would have been shamed.

For the community, his looking out for the son would have made it worse. You can imagine his neighbours saying to each other, 'Have you seen that silly old fool, hanging around looking for that useless son of his? Hasn't he learned anything? You would have thought he had more self-respect.'

When the son comes back it all gets worse. The father runs, something that important people are often too dignified to do. He embraces the son.[2] He honours him with a ring on his hand, a sign of familial authority, with a cloak, a sign of wealth, with shoes, a sign of status, and above all with a top-class feast for all. When Jesus was telling the story, it is possible to imagine that the crowd – on hearing that the father was looking out for and ran towards his son – would have expected the story to continue something like: 'He beat him, kicked him, rebuked him, but out of great kindness offered him a role in the house as the lowest form of slave.' How much more astonished would they have been at the way the story unfolded.

Many of us have a sneaking sense of sympathy for the older brother. What he says is true. He has done the right thing and yet he has not been rewarded for it. Capital has been taken out of the family farm that could have been invested and was instead squandered. His father has been moping around on the road in a probably fruitless wait for the return of the prodigal. And when it does happen the old man throws a lavish party, so loud that the elder son can hear it as he comes in from the fields. It is no wonder that he is furious.

With the older brother there is the same sacrifice of dignity by the father. Instead of ordering him to come in, join the party and at least try to look pleased, he goes out and begs him to come in. It was the older brother's job to reconcile, but he does not. It was his role to set an example of respect for his father, but he does not.

Jesus is speaking to two groups. He is saying to those who have wandered from God, 'Come back; whatever you have done, you are loved by God, not just as servants but as children.' He is saying to the religious leaders, 'Come in and feast on the goodness of God, of which you already know, but seem to have forgotten. You too are loved; receive that love and with it these prodigals who have found their way back to God.'

Biblical approaches to reconciliation are decisive and clear, based in actions that both symbolize and enact reconciliation. The process takes time and sometimes fails, but begins with a marked point. In the Prodigal Son passage, both the speech and the acts of the Father are powerful testimonies to his forgiveness. The psychological subtleties are not overlooked but the order of events and symbols is different from our more gradualist approach in the Global North, where forgiveness is at the end of the process. God starts with forgiving.

In most disputes the greatest risk to the facilitators is being insulted, mistrusted and disliked. Motives will be doubted. Actions will be second-guessed. It requires resilience and the moral imagination to continue and through love to demonstrate to all parties that the objective is peace, and that true, just peace is a feast worth anything.

In situations of armed conflict, taking physical risk is also essential. No facilitator or peacebuilder going into a conflict area takes the same risks as those who live there all the time. Usually, it will not even be the same risk as to the diplomats stationed in the area, or the relief personnel from NGOs and multilateral agencies such as the UN. But to go there makes all the difference. It gives credibility that when many have gone the opposite way someone came to be alongside, even if only briefly. The unique significance of Jesus Christ begins with God taking flesh, incarnation. Fully God and fully human, Jesus endured all the troubles of living in a very troubled part of the world. He came to share our humanity so as to make it possible for us to share his eternal life.

RISK FOR THOSE IN THE DISPUTE

Yet if we love those in the dispute and seek their flourishing, the aspect of risk that weighs most heavily is the one that they face.

This is the risk of the consequences of decisions. Actions and omissions have consequences, and once past the events of the action or omission, the consequences will come in one way or another. They may be mitigated or changed, but other things will have to happen as a result of what we do and don't do.

The actions of the industrial revolutions and of the growth in economies, energy use, global wealth, technologies and populations over the last two hundred years or so have the consequence of global warming, loss of biodiversity and threats to the circumstances and even in some cases existence of those who will be alive in the late twenty-first century. Some of those consequences are already very present indeed. We cannot undo the actions, and as each year passes, we cannot undo the inactions that have been allowed.

It seems obvious but it is easily forgotten. As I mentioned in the Introduction, a UK strategic outlook in 2021 spoke of the policy around the use of nuclear weapons. It never said anything about the policy for the aftermath of using nuclear weapons. But there would have to be one. Actions have consequences, but it is very human to avoid thinking them through.

In armed conflict a risk of beginning a process of reconciliation is the loss of impetus in seeking victory. A second risk is loss of confidence in the leader's commitment. What Churchill felt in 1940 is that any politician who sought terms of peace would be thrown out of office on the spot and replaced by someone with greater determination.

There are some circumstances where resistance, even armed resistance, is the only possible response to forces so evil that no negotiation is possible. Most people see 1940 as one of those. However, we must bear in mind that the early steps towards conflict begin with demonizing the opponent. That happened in 1914, with terrible results. In George Orwell's *1984* the enemies are all demonized, without challenge. The result is eternal conflict and tyranny. We have to acknowledge that few – but some – groups are intrinsically evil. Most are mixtures, hence the need for research and relationships.

The moral imagination of alternatives to conflict will often be a crucial part of the work of the facilitator, but it must be offered as a gift, not imposed, and it must be done in a way that builds on research, relationships and relief work. Yet the consequences of the exercise of the moral imagination increase the risk levels in the process. At the same time, the absence of any exercise of moral imagination almost certainly condemns the process to failure. The facilitator is on a road where a new map has to be drawn, a map that itself helps to create the topography through which the participants journey. However, once started, the option of stopping and ceasing to move while the map is drawn is not usually a possibility. The consequences of starting a reconciliation process is to follow the road either where the participants were going or on a new route that they themselves imagine: there is rarely a third option. Actions have consequences.

I have always found that two equal and equally unpalatable risks present themselves at some point during every facilitation. One is to meet and the other is not to meet.

Of course, 'meeting' is a concept with many shapes. Bringing together those who were in dispute used to be a process of literally sitting in the same room. The advent of new forms of communication offers far more choice and opportunity for a sliding scale of risk in the encounter. This is yet to be proved, but increasingly facilitators are reporting that a video conference meeting can be much more carefully calibrated than physical presence. It is also harder to walk out of. I once did quit a meeting on video conference, making a dramatic exit, as I thought. The drama was diminished and my sense of foolishness rightly increased when it turned out that half the meeting thought my connection had gone down.

Meetings may either be remote, which removes the difficult negotiations on where and how to meet, or adjoining but separate. In this case there is a sort of shuttle diplomacy in which the facilitator goes from one group to another. It is less confrontational but also very significantly less effective.

In the end the day has to come when real human beings in dispute meet in the same physical space to seek to imagine a new future. Unless it is a form of dispute in which the settlement will end all contact definitively, the outcome of a successful start to the process will be growing contact and the need to live with one another as the parties develop the future they have begun to imagine.

As an example, let us return to the issue of climate change and global warming. The paradox of meetings is that they involve huge numbers of people flying around the world in exactly the forms of transport that contribute to the thing they are seeking to prevent. As a result, and because of the COVID-19 pandemic, the proportion of meeting being done online has gone up enormously. Yet their impact is limited. Whatever steps are progressively put in place, or not as the case may be, the world will have to live together with the consequences. This conflict between the climate and the human population is by far and away the most complicated one to resolve in human history. Yet it *is* a conflict, and one reason for the long delays in confronting it is that it is only now being recognized as such. I have deliberately included the question of reconciliation with both climate and the innumerable parties to the conflict as an example, because reconciliation is required for necessary action to be taken.

First, one party is not human: the climate and the biosphere. It is the weaker party in the short term, suffering the consequences of human acts and omissions. Yet, in the long term the climate will dominate. What happens to it is in the end a matter of science, but it is science that is not understood in its detail. It is now generally accepted that global warming is caused overwhelmingly by human beings. It is not known exactly how, or to what extent, the process may have other influences, and whether self-reinforcing feedback loops are already playing a role. Even definitions of targets such as 'zero-carbon' can be argued about. So, although we have mainly moved as a human race from unconscious ignorance, we are still in many areas in conscious ignorance or at best very partial knowledge.

Second, the conflict map is incomplete in identifying the different interests and needs of all the millions of parties involved. The map has vast blank areas where it is hard to assess who the actors are, who the spoilers are and who will shift from being in one category to another owing to extraneous or short-term issues relating to other conflicts, to trade, to political change or to entirely unforeseeable impacts of economic collapse, wars or events like the pandemic.

Third, questions of ethics arise as to who can carry a burden – and how – the size of which we cannot yet accurately measure. Yet, the choice of pausing and waiting does not exist, because inaction is itself a decision with consequences that we do know, and that we are aware cannot be supported by a significant proportion of the world.

Fourth, there is not yet agreement on relief needs, nor on how to meet them. Disasters are handled ad hoc, whether it be flooding, storms or droughts.

The risk of meeting is therefore huge. A failed meeting would be a colossal setback that might in the end derail the whole process. Yet not to meet regularly, albeit that the meetings' outcomes are exceptionally difficult to manage, would be the greater disaster. At the meetings, the rich look the poor in the eye and hear first-hand the tales of struggle and suffering. The heart can be touched as well as the mind. The sciences can be assisted by the graces of compassion and fellow feeling.

The same pattern of analysis can be made of anything from family disputes to wars, community struggles to commercial litigation. Both meeting and not meeting are each a risky choice.

MITIGATING RISK

Risk raises key questions. First, who is best able to carry the risk? And second, how can it be made less severe?

There are a number of approaches to the first question, but one model put forward is the Risk Allocation Matrix (RAM).

Let us use an imaginary case. The Diocese of Barchester[3] is in great difficulty. The dean of the cathedral and the bishop have fallen out badly and both brought complaints against each other. The dean accuses the bishop of sexist behaviour, of sexual harassment and of bullying the dean's staff. She (the dean) has been off work with stress, and the cathedral congregation, which is very disconnected from the diocese, is sympathetic to her. The bishop has a pattern of falling out with staff. Nevertheless, he inherited a diocese that was on the edge of financial insolvency, where numbers of those attending church were collapsing, where recruiting clergy was nearly impossible, and where only a very small minority of the ones in post thought prayer and worship to be of any significance. The average Diocesan Synod was like the House of Commons without the same level of charity.

The Archbishop of Wessex is in despair (although to be fair he is such a long streak of misery on a good day that it is hard to tell the difference). He has asked for mediation and reconciliation work to be done.

The facilitator and team have begun work with nearly a hundred meetings across the diocese, collated on the church equivalent of Scotland Yard's Holmes system for managing complex cases and linking up disparate areas of evidence. In this case it is called Father Brown (FB) after Chesterton's detective.[4] As a result, they have discovered a pattern of bad and autocratic decisions and lack of communication leading to a breakdown of trust going back to the nineteenth century and a bishop's chaplain called Slope.

Having gained the confidence of many people at the grassroots and in the leadership of diocese and county, and with the help of FB identifying common themes, they have begun to meet certain needs, with the help of central church funding. The diocese has received a grant to pay salaries, there is an internal communications expert on loan, the dean is receiving counselling and the bishop is getting coaching. It is time for the senior staff and the key leaders to begin a process of cascading meetings to see a way forward.

What if it all goes wrong? Here is a very simplified form of the RAM.

	Bishop	Clergy	Laity	Cathedral	Central Church Funds
Loss of confidence within diocese	Too autocratic to deal with it	With encouragement and help can renew prayer life and inspire laity	Wonderful but need good inspiration. Local lay ministry?	Too fragile	Irrelevant to risk
Insolvency	Able to talk to Central Church Funds	Can manage locally but cannot all handle raising money for stipend payments	Pandemic has cut giving	Broke	Has reserves for this purpose
Public disagreement worsens	Persuadable to share in an event of repentance and reconciliation	Too dispersed	Too dispersed	Willing to try as a place for a renewal of common life	Not relevant
Senior staff breakup	Archbishop of Wessex would need to deal with bishop	Big danger of splitting	Big danger of splitting	Unable to respond	Can find and support interim staff

Of course, Barchester is not part of the Church of England or any other church group at all, and any appearance of similarity to any diocese outside the nineteenth-century books of Anthony Trollope is purely coincidental. In addition, this is very simplified. Most people would see it differently.

The aim of the RAM is that, before meeting, the principal foreseeable risks are set out and there is an analysis of which party or which outsider will be most influential for good or ill and how that risk will be faced. Who can handle the consequences, who cannot? The RAM can be made more and more complicated but is best kept to the point where it does not give answers but does ask the central questions about how to manage the risk of meeting. There can be a lead RAM that summarizes and there can be sub-matrices for different areas. Actions to be taken can be added. It is a flexible tool.

Mitigating risk involves developing resilience among those involved in the dispute, so that the process is not toppled over by a setback. Resilience will come from the moral imagination, from relationships and from developing a sense of hope. It is above all a question of confidence and the facilitation team must all be as one in expressing publicly the expectation that there is a way forward, however difficult.

Risk is also mitigated by the way meetings are set up. I remember missing this point some years ago and arriving at a meeting to address the claims of a group that they had been left out. The meeting was conducted in the normal way (a serious error) and the unhappy group were sat on one side and told they should only speak if spoken to. The whole set-up confirmed that they were being left out and it was a serious setback.

Generous hospitality and humility by the hosts is essential. As was written in Chapter 2, remember the body. Adequate ventilation, clear sight-lines, a space for the acoustics so that everyone can hear easily, suitable food, and comfortable chairs that do not encourage sleep will all help. If people have travelled, give them time to recover. Beautiful surroundings, good music, a regular timetable that is kept to, and a capacity to be in touch with others will quieten nerves. If the conflict is centred in a place of different faiths, make equal room for prayer, contemplation and silence for all, in a way that is appropriate to them. Do everything you can to respect the different faith communities' habits or dietary rules. Care for the details. That shows love.

Above all, do not spring surprises. People will need to know exactly what to expect, from the largest to the smallest aspect.

The next chapter will bring in some of the absolute essential values in peacebuilding, most importantly truth and justice.

Summary

- Creating a fork in a road that otherwise leads only towards deepening hatred and further confrontation requires the moral imagination of which Lederach writes so powerfully. Normally a reconciliation process will require many such forks in a road that is otherwise heading only for confrontation.
- Each fork is a place of meeting or decision or both, and thus of risk.

- There are risks for the facilitators. These will involve emotional and psychological strains, the acceptance of not being trusted and, in some situations, physical dangers. All must necessarily be faced.
- There are even greater risks for those in the confrontation. A failed process is a huge blow and often makes things worse.
- It is essential to see what the risks are for all involved, who is most capable of carrying them and who is least capable.
- Risk mitigation is a question of detailed work as well as careful thinking. It comes down to making people feel deeply secure and equally valued.

POINTS TO PONDER

- What are the issues in a conflict that make you most uncomfortable? Is it raised voices? Silence? Threats? Being mistrusted? Or any other things? How will you find resilience to cope with these discomforts in any area of reconciliation and peacebuilding?
- When you look at conflicts and disagreements about which you know, at any level, what are the risks you identify with an absence of progress in reconciliation or attempting reconciliation?
- Consider from your own experience what makes you most able to relax and be open about what is on your mind. Think about the physical, the emotional, the psychological and the spiritual factors.

- Finally, ask yourself how those sorts of things can be applied in tense situations. What will set a meeting on the road towards feeling sufficiently safe?

Case Study (continued)

See if you can develop a RAM for the St Thomas dispute (see page 118). Enter 'Risks' in the left-hand column, the names of groups or individuals across the top. The key questions are about developing a sense of who is strong and who is weak, who can bear which risks and who can't. The conclusion that you are seeking is: 'What meetings might I have; with whom, and how?' Who is not in the story who should be? Who do you need to get onside? Which VIPs locally might help as conveners? Put yourselves in the shoes of each group and use your imagination to empathize. There are few simple right or wrongs here.

8

Reconciling – the Long Journey

Having Researched, built Relationships, begun a programme of Relieving need with partners suited for whatever the need is, taken a deep breath and, after careful thought, Risked the beginning of meeting, the long journey of Reconciling can now move into the next phase.

It is worth going back to what reconciliation is and is not. Reconciliation is a portfolio word meaning the gathering together of all the processes and skills necessary to transform destructive differences and conflicts into constructive and imaginative acceptance of difference and capacity to disagree well.

Reconciliation is not a series of compromises to reach a weak middle ground on which all stand, equally unhappily and with no basis for action together. That is kicking the can down the road, or into the long grass or wherever. Fuzziness of that sort is the evasion of the challenge of difference. What should be sought is a transparent and clear-eyed blessing and welcome of diversity so that all, without exception, may have an equal opportunity to flourish as individuals and groups. Reconciliation is also, especially, not the signing of a peace agreement or some other kind of accord, and assuming 'that is that, deal done, problem solved'.

If we compare the last two paragraphs it is easy to see why reconciliation, properly understood, is so difficult and takes so long.

At its heart is the transformation of every part of a person and group.

There will be a need to see some opponents differently, at least the ones who are themselves willing to be involved in the process. Seeing people and groups differently is not necessarily seeing them as good but, at the least, as people with whom to engage if possible.

There will be a need to forgo some aspects of the conflict, especially violence or its threat and other forms of deeply destructive behaviour. The process will have to lead to a change of heart as well as commitment to the journey. Changing hearts takes a very long time even in the simplest of cases. It is difficult and demanding for all involved.

There will need to be a fresh approach to justice, and a realistic search for truth. Myths will be exposed. Long-held assumptions will be progressively changed by continued contact and relationship building. A dispute that has naturally focused on what was objectionable about the other may well begin to change into a more or less friendly partnership looking outwards to the world around and seeking to bless it.

It is an uncertain process. It has moments of failure and despair and success and elation. It is prone to fits and starts, to forgetfulness and to recalling its importance. The further away in time that the destructive confrontations become, the less urgency there is in reconciliation. It may collapse altogether for a while, or look as if it has collapsed.

So once the engagement with the other has started, what are the key elements?

The most important question is about how to approach the demands of conflicted parties for truth and justice. They are also the most controversial parts of reconciliation. That is why handling those issues comes at this point and not earlier. They come later because they are so important that there has to have been a solid establishment of relationships evidenced by taking risks in meeting, the relief of need, and founded in good and continuing research. Otherwise, both truth and justice become weaponized by one side or the other or both.

The very action of introducing these areas will raise the risk level a great deal more, but ignoring them is the kiss of death. There can never be reconciliation unless it is clear that the journey involves addressing injustices and seeking to find a common understanding of events. However, how they are handled is itself very difficult to manage.

OPENING TRUTH – REVEALING MYTH

The hunt for any sort of knowledge begins with asking the right questions and using the right approach about what is being hunted. You do not look for new stars with a microscope, nor is a telescope of much value in seeking the answers to the makeup of the ocean floor.

Each conflict will have its own myths, and the longer they have gone on, the more embedded they become. 'Truths' that were recognized as convenient myths when first put forward end up as articles of dogma in the hands of supporters of one view.

That is very clearly seen in responses to the conflict in the UK and USA over racism, and in the UK especially over the legacies of slavery. It is one of the most necessary issues to face and will need long work, probably over decades. It reveals itself in different views of history, particularly that of the British Empire, and in rapidly accepted statements of so-called truth. For example, the title of the violence within the army of the East India Company (EIC) beginning in 1857 together with many simultaneous conflicts within Princely States is referred to very often in the UK as the Indian Mutiny, but in India it is called by a variety of other names including the First War of Independence, or the Uprising. For many years these later titles were rejected as it was argued that India was too disparate to have a single war of independence at that stage and that the British-ruled area was an oasis of order. However, that view is widely challenged by contemporary evidence of letters gathered by Indian and British historians, and indeed the demonstration that the British were seen as a common menace, a source of economic destruction and far from benevolent, dates back as far as the late eighteenth century.[1]

That may seem a long time ago. Yet, for any process of building relationships between modern India and the modern UK, the question of a serious search for the truth will be essential. Memories matter and symbols change thinking. Visiting Amritsar in 2019 I was taken to see the site of an infamous massacre of Indians by British troops in 1919, at a place called Jallianwala Bagh. The killings were the result of the troops opening fire on an unarmed crowd at close range when there was nowhere for the crowd to flee. It was a horrifying atrocity. When I came to the memorial to those who had died, I prostrated myself before it. That caused much fuss in the UK, but in India it was seen as a gesture of deep sorrow, owing to the historical significance of prostration.

Another very current example is that of the island of Ireland. During a trip to Dublin, also in 2019, I was astonished by the impact of a state visit there by Queen Elizabeth II in 2011, as a contribution to reconciliation after the Troubles of the late twentieth century in Northern Ireland. Every detail was recalled to me, particularly the recognition by the Queen of the troubled history between England and Ireland, her speaking in Irish at the beginning of a speech, her visiting memorials to Irish Republicans, and other apparently more mundane but for the Irish very significant gestures, including the bright green of her dress.

Her visit had a huge impact at the time. Its perceptive use of symbol reflected a step forward in the discussions of historical truth, and an acknowledgement that the past was much more complicated than it was often allowed to appear.

It is a good example because the truth in Northern Ireland remains highly contentious. In July 2021 there were exchanges in the UK Parliament about the legacy of the troubles and the very difficult issue of accountability for such events as the Bloody Sunday killings in Londonderry/Derry (even the name has very significant political connotations arising from history). The history even of the extremely well-documented recent past is contested on nearly every point.

The reality of every dispute is that the truth that is sought will always be affected by the point at which one starts and the lenses one has.

This can easily lead to a sense of despair or of relativism in which the rightful assumption that an absolute and agreed sense of the truth in a dispute is impossible to reach leads to the wrongful conclusion that no search for truth is worth undertaking.

Truth in terms of telling a true story can be progressively uncovered by many small steps. Like the buried cities of Pompeii and Herculaneum, continued excavation reveals more and more and enables a clearer picture of the overall pattern of life.

One of the best examples of progressive and helpful truth telling was in the South African Truth and Reconciliation Commission. Detailed examination of testimony was both politically illuminating and enabled the culture of the Apartheid state to be revealed.[2]

The nature of conflictual relationships is that there is always a fear that facilitators are falling for the stories told by others. In a marriage dispute, one will often hear that the mediator, the judge, the lawyers, the social workers all believed the other party, for example the husband. Yet all the wife's friends believed her, and one is told that thus everyone else was fooled. Even in the terrible cases of the abuse of children and vulnerable adults there will be passionate defences of the perpetrator, not just when suspicions first arise, but also after they have been formally accused, and even after legal and police action.

The facilitator's approach to truth will therefore always be cautious but persistent.

First, in any large-scale dispute the reconciliation process must include truth discovery by people who have no skin in the game. In a community, this may well be the mediator in the dispute, who listens carefully. In a relationship, the relationship counsellor will do it. As the scale becomes larger or more complicated it will become necessary to build up partnerships, with anything from forensic accounting, where large sums of money are at stake, to specialist historians who are known in the relevant field.

Three examples illustrate the point about the difficulties.

In the Ogoni example and in the wider conflicts in the Niger Delta, already described, good progress was made long after I had moved on by the use of environmental programmes to assess the damage caused and to oversee the discussions about reparations. One Commission in Bayelsa State was led by the then Archbishop of York, now Lord Sentamu, with powerful effect. The clarity brought to the different accounts of environmental degradation contributed to the possibility of setting up a fund and commissioning work in the wetlands.

Second, in one area where I worked, historical enquiry indicated that a very serious outbreak of violence, which was initially described as Christian vs Muslim, had significant roots in ethnic rivalries. For some time, there was an improvement, which has now been reversed as a result of more general conflict in the country concerned. This is an example of where truth is strongly contested. For those involved, the issue of Christian against Muslim is easy to understand, mobilizes internal support and generates external sponsorship from overseas observers in one way or another. Religion certainly plays a significant part, but there are also historical rivalries and the introduction of a new factor in terms of climate change driving people movements.

The reaction from those whose external support depended on the religious conflict message was understandably to deny any complexity beyond the

Christian/Muslim factors, and allege either persecution by Muslims or persecution by Christians. In any peacebuilding process, participants must be listened to as perception is almost as important as reality. In the first place, perception *is* the reality they feel that they experience, and, second, no peace will be built unless there is the beginning of a process of movement towards a common story. In other words, start where people are in terms of truth, not where the facilitator feels they ought to be. Recognize that statements of facts are necessary but far from sufficient, and will be challenged, even irrationally. The impact of narrative on brain chemistry, emotions and thus responses is also foundational. Movements to change the narrative affect the whole physiology of individuals and thus groups, especially those in leadership. They respond with flight or flight, and the handling of truth discovery thus must 'remember the body'.

Incidentally, as so often, in the case just described the mention of factors other than religion earned the facilitator a great deal of abuse from everyone. Other factors were threatening to all sides in that they undermined their self-identity as victims. In a study of the issues of shame and honour in Palestine and Israel a powerful comment was: 'Without the expectation of vindication, the role of the righteous victim risks losing its face-saving function. It could easily take on qualities of the weakling, the deserving victim or, worse, one who condones wickedness.'[3] We cannot forget the intense importance of shame and honour in conflict.

Third, in the UK the issue of racial justice, especially as it affects people of Caribbean and African heritage, is one where truth is hard to pin down. Cover up of the terrible abuses of the Windrush scandal,[4] a lack of welcome in churches and other institutions, institutional racism and many other failings obscured the realities of life for Black people in the UK.

After the murder of George Floyd in the USA in the middle of 2020, the challenge of institutional racism and Whiteness or White privilege resurfaced, especially among the Black population and among young people of colour more than in other groups. At the same time there was pushback from White groups and a number of highly confrontational and even violent clashes in London and other places across the country.

Within the Church of England other incidents spiralled to cause a great loss of confidence by not only Black but other ethnic minority members, especially those who are ordained or in the process of training or of discerning a call to ordination. Memories of past experiences were reawakened.

A leading member of the Black Majority churches (mostly Pentecostal in tradition) in the UK organized a series of online conferences with Black church leaders, youth leaders and young people from across the Christian tradition. It was attended by four of the presidents of Churches Together in England, including myself.

The encounters were remarkable and testing. The experience of the young Black leaders was of continually being stopped and searched, of a sense of profound alienation in a White country where Whiteness is the controlling dynamic in most institutions, including churches. I spoke at the same time to a remarkable and exceptional Black priest in the Church of England. They confirmed the impression of racism, which held despite that particular person being in a senior role and being widely recognized for their work. Their perception was of a 'cultural disorder' where Whiteness is in everything that is done. They saw change as involving both power and truth. They were utterly demoralized by their experience.

While I was hearing this, I was also talking to senior police officers of different ethnic backgrounds and to politicians in government and opposition. Again, there was no agreement on truth, although they saw the issue as very important and believed strongly in the idea of truth. More than that, they were convinced that their view was true. The police were not, as a number of officers saw it, harassing young Black men; they were seeking to stop knife crime, which had a disproportionate number of Black victims. They were aiming to protect, not persecute.

The argument continues to sway to and fro. That is for further along in this book. The reality of the disagreement among most people cannot be put down to malice but is a question of different perceptions that are related and believed — genuinely, sincerely, deeply and without malice — as being the whole truth; not a part of the truth that their opponents refuse to accept. There may be a minority that seeks confrontation and trouble, but it is not the general rule.

Progress will take time but needs to be made. It cannot wait until, as if by a miracle, everyone wakes up one morning with the same perception. The capacity to own a narrative, or to live with multiple narratives and yet be in relationships, albeit with grave and painful struggles, will be a mark of the transformation of reconciliation. It will be very far from the finished product, but it will help.

Even in reading that last paragraph we each come to it with different eyes. For the minority communities, the struggle to get to the truth is not just painful, it is existential. Many, not all, feel dehumanized, dismissed as

a reality in society. It is immensely important to recognize
that reconciliation begins with sacrifice, and sacrifice
is the responsibility of the stronger, majority, groups,
not the obligation of those who are already victims.
For many White people, who are themselves ignored
and marginalized by economic, educational and social
circumstances, to speak of them as privileged is rightly
heard as patronizing nonsense. The complexity of the
fragile human condition and the myriad characteristics
we hold mean that life is not a simple binary or a game
of snakes and ladders. While we may not always be
vulnerable to marginalization and oppressive conditions
by virtue of a particular condition, this does not make us
invulnerable in other spheres.

Embracing complexity means precision. Black Lives
Matter is not all Black people against all White people.
White people are not a single category, any more than
those of UK minority (but global majority) ethnic
heritage. They are all first and foremost people, human
beings, to be treated with equal dignity and not to be
patronized, ignored or put in a category. That is a good
place to start.

Justice Delayed Can Be Justice Affirmed

It is a great gift to live in a place where the administration
of justice is genuinely intended to be neutral and
unswayed by political considerations, albeit with very
human failings. The corruption of the courts, or their
capture by one group, is the first and most necessary step
towards ending democracy and freedom of speech.[5] In
mid-2021 severe riots broke out across South Africa after
the imprisoning of the former president, Jacob Zuma,

for refusing to pay attention to the courts. Although it was very disruptive, cost many lives and damaged the economy, the ability of the court to prevail was widely seen as a good step for democracy. By contrast, the Chinese Communist Party declares that independent courts are a threat to party rule and thus to the good of the country.

The need for an independent and apolitical judiciary is based deeply in the realities of human beings. The use of power almost always leads to the abuse of power. Those who wish for an outcome to their policies will sooner or later begin to see that outcome as the just result and any other as unjust.

Yet justice is fragile; it flourishes in strong light but wilts in darkness, and is easily killed in times of conflict. Victor's justice is always a great fear. The winners of a war apportion 'justice' against the losers without giving attention to proper representation, and when the 'justice' is in the midst of conflict, violent or not, it will be far more likely to have the characteristics of revenge.

Justice must therefore be independent and must wait for the moments when people are confident that it is being done calmly.

Institutions are especially bad at the administration of justice within their own systems. The nature of an institution is to seek to preserve its life. Those who end up leading an institution are likely to see survival of that institution as best guaranteed by their own survival as leaders.[6] One might imagine the Bishop of Barchester channelling the future head of General Motors and saying to himself, 'What is good for me is good for the Diocese of Barchester.' A state of co-dependency is created that can only be broken by independence in justice, and yet the sense of self-protection is so great a power that almost any reason can be found for preserving internal control.

To be bad at justice within one's own system will lead to being bad at justice wherever one has power. Add to the human desire for power the stresses and tensions of dispute, let alone violent conflict, and there will be an overwhelming tendency towards injustice.

The slogan (and title of an NGO), 'No Peace Without Justice', is thus accurate only with a series of provisos. They include that the justice must be independent of the most powerful, and committed to impartiality, and at the right time, which will almost always be once conditions of the dispute have calmed, as a means of avoiding a new flare-up. Theologically, Christianity claims that sometimes good justice will only be found before God and is beyond human reach. That may be the case where a perpetrator cannot be found, or the truth seems unfathomable. It is not a reason for human effort to end: it is a source of eternal hope.

John's Gospel, chapter 21, has an aura of peace and of resolution, but that is a surprise. It takes place only a few weeks after the chaos, betrayal and cowardice of the disciples at the arrest and crucifixion of Jesus. The disciples are still coming to terms with the idea that he rose from the dead and has appeared to them. Resurrection life, which he has given them through breathing the Holy Spirit into them, is to be lived in the ordinary. It is not living on a continuous elevated plane slightly disconnected from the world. Food needs buying, families and friends need feeding. Peter tells his friends that he is going fishing in the Sea of Galilee. This is not, as some commentators suggest, an attempt to return to his life before meeting Jesus; it is getting on with things.

Yet, even among the disciples and certainly with Peter, there must have been a lurking cloud. They had not stood by Jesus. Jesus has not mentioned this to date, but it is there, an elephant by the lake, to misuse a cliché. After a fruitless night of fishing without catching, the power of the narrative comes in waves of ever deeper love from Jesus, waves that ever more powerfully commission them for the rest of their lives.

First, a stranger on the shore calls out instructing them where to place their nets. The voice will have been clear in the early morning stillness. The net is filled with fish. All of them will immediately have remembered, as we do as John's readers, the story of the great catch of fish at the beginning of the ministry of Jesus.[7] They have been recommissioned, reconciled after their failure, not in some messy compromise but in the power of the grace of God catching them and reimagining their futures.

Then, when they have all got to the shore, they find breakfast made. Again, this takes them back to the feeding of the five thousand and, through there, to the feeding of the Israelites during the Exodus by God in the wilderness. Jesus' reconciliation relieves their hunger and assures them that his promise that those who follow him will not hunger – spiritually – is true. The reconciliation has moved on from renewal of relationship in hospitality, the meeting of need and the security of being in God's hands.

Finally, Peter is taken aside, and in three questions his denial of Jesus at the time of Jesus' arrest is reversed. Justice is done, truth is revealed. Peter does not have failure swept under the carpet but rather it is clearly exposed, truthfully addressed and justly dealt with, by the perfectly just God who has shown Peter what it is to fail and be restored.

Truth and justice are met in love, and the result is healing and a future.

TRUTH AND JUSTICE – SOURCES OF HOPE

Truth and justice are central to the character of God in what we see by God being revealed through Jesus. Wisdom in timing, in place and in manner of dealing with sin and failure puts them in a context of safety and security, not a context of uncertainty and revenge. That has to be true of any process of reconciliation, even more so once we take account of the fragilities of human nature, of our proclivity to confuse justice with what we want, and truth with what we perceive.

The facilitator – however large and complicated or small and simple the dispute, whether it has the violence of guns or the savagery of words and hatreds – has to take as a central aim the establishment of a 'Galilee beach': a place of peace and security where truth and justice are seen and recognized.

MAINTAINING THE MOMENTUM

All that having been said, the issue of maintaining the momentum and excitement of the journey of peacebuilding will continually come back.

I have been using the metaphor of a journey. In 1977 or so two friends and I walked across Scotland from the Kyle of Lochalsh to Montrose, sea to sea. It was a long and beautiful walk across the Highlands, camping in remote valleys. It was also very enjoyable apart from the midges and blisters. When I look back more than forty years on, there are various moments that stick in my mind, milestones that enable me to see how we kept going (a fourth person did drop out).

The journey of reconciliation is a very long walk indeed. I remember a married couple I knew whose marriage disintegrated. They separated and began the process of divorce. In a series of remarkable events, they got back together, despite one having found a new partner, and cancelled the divorce at the very last moment.

There will be many who would have loved that to have been true for themselves, but I am not holding this couple up as especially virtuous, any more than they claimed to be so. That is not the point of the story. Some years after they got back together, I was chatting to one of them and asked how they were. 'It takes a lot of working out,' was the reply. Long journeys take a lot of working out. On our Scottish walk we had Ordnance Survey maps and compasses (no satellite navigation in those days). Milestones were important — they gave a lift — but the dogged hard work was reading the map, getting the direction right and putting one foot in front of another on agonizingly steep hills where it felt as though some nasty person had added several bricks to the backpack.

Much reconciliation and peacebuilding work is patiently sitting in a hot room trying to get the direction right. I want to suggest a number of ways of keeping the momentum in the hard work as well as in the high moments.

Tell the Story Forwards and Backwards

In Part I the two dangers of overspeed and overreach were discussed. One of the methods of containing them is to set realistic and achievable targets while maintaining as a final aim the vision of the sunny uplands that are the ultimate destination.

A way of forming the vision and getting the general direction established uses working together to develop the moral imagination of a world without the conflict, the imagination of a 'golden age' and then the development of a backwards history process to look from the future and see how you got there.

At its heart it is an attempt to draw people into a common story and permit the surfacing of what they see as ideals. If a secure enough environment can be created in the discussions, by small groups and lots of preparation and briefing, those involved are asked to look forward perhaps five or maybe ten years, to two imagined scenarios.

One is a dark age when everything has gone wrong. They are asked to describe it and to set out in some detail what it is that makes it so bad.

The other scenario is a golden age when their best hopes are fulfilled. Once again, they are asked to describe it and say why it is so good.

The second linked exercise is to take the future situations they have imagined, and to fill in the intervening time with the actions and omissions that happened to get to those places. This is the history backwards. Stand in the future scenario that has been imagined and tell the story of how it happened, year by year.

These exercises work best in lower-level and informal disputes, in a community or a church setting. At the level of conflict, they may come in useful later, but the expectations of face-to-face negotiation will be very high. It will almost certainly be necessary to mix and match different approaches as the exhaustion of face-to-face talks often leads to a loss of the sense of direction and desire for the future, and participants become intransigent.

To do these exercises properly will take days for a complicated situation and much less for a simple one. It needs to wait until those in the different groups are sufficiently relaxed with each other to be able to risk a level of openness. The exercises should be repeated occasionally to enable participants to see the progress that is being made and to refine their ideas.

Probably there will be little interaction between the different sides at the beginning. It may be necessary to do the first round entirely separately so that they can each discover more about the others. The expectation and experience are that they grow into an ability to work together in their imaginations, as a first step to working together in reality.

These exercises are sensitive and difficult to time, to design and to moderate. There will always be objections to 'playing games' and part of the facilitators' skills are going to be shown in the pace, the layout and design of the process, and how to ensure that its use is communicated and accepted.

Facilitators will also introduce the very serious questions for consideration. The history backwards exercise will need to include the ways in which truth and justice were established and by what mechanisms.

The underlying purpose of the exercises is to make space for the moral imagination. The question for each side is: 'What would a truly good society look like?' At the beginning, the answer from every side is very likely to be: 'One in which we are in total control.' The introduction of further questions, the mixing in of direct talks and time spent in imagining the future and the ways forward will remind participants of what they are seeking, enable unrealistic goals (e.g. complete victory) to be challenged, and open the way to non-binding discussions of what is good, preparing the way for the decisions emerging from negotiations.

RUNNING ON PARALLEL LINES

The idea of truth and reconciliation commissions almost always appears at some point. Like the exercises just mentioned, they are enormously powerful tools, but seldom of value by themselves. They are the best known of a wide range of approaches, the timing of which is very delicate, and if used either too early or too late will become useless or even destructive.

Imagine a railway line, single track. If there is a blockage everything stops. The blockage can be a broken rail (easily repaired), a landslide (takes time to deal with but not complicated), a bridge down (major problem). There may be traffic coming both ways, meaning one has to give ground (not at all easy). A simple answer is to run more than one track, but with points to connect them. There will still be blockages, but there will be a great deal more flexibility in dealing with them.

A community dispute is likely to involve many people. There will be leaders, supporters, encouragers, opponents, some elected, some informal, some belonging to organizations with community power such as residents' associations, schools, hospitals and churches. The dispute might be over access to community facilities, or their absence, or new housing, or a bypass, or any number of other questions.

Facilitating such a dispute in one gathering is likely to be very difficult. Blockages will result from groups feeling left out in a big meeting. There will be discrimination against more vulnerable groups that have difficulty in expressing themselves. The strong will dominate. The development of parallel tracks in which blockages that could affect the main line can be dealt with before they become serious is a way both of managing a difficult level of complexity and a wide variety of levels of power and of keeping a sense of momentum. There will always be something happening. In this approach the biggest and highest-level meeting will focus on key issues and should arrive with a good level of participation and many potential tangles already straightened out. Communication of all that is going on will be essential, for the suspicions of a community that is locked into a dispute will always be of deals being done and fixes being fixed behind the back of other people.

The number of tracks will vary very considerably according to the number of groups that have opposing views, and that need to be able to sort a way forward. Each track requires facilitation, and each track will gain expectations of being important. The balance between creating inclusion and adding superfluous complexity is very difficult to manage.

Inclusion matters. Deals done on high without a top-down, middle-out, bottom-up approach will lack approval and thus fail to gain a social licence to operate in practice. Grassroots deals will be subsumed in overall, elite-based conflict. Those who can wield a power of veto and have an interest in the dispute continuing will do so unless there is significant grassroots pressure that overwhelms obstructions.

Truth and Reconciliation Commissions (TRCs)

These have been discussed in principle elsewhere. The questions in practice are simple to ask and very hard to answer. The answer to the first question must be no and to the others must be yes.

- Is a TRC being looked at as a magic wand that will make everything suddenly better?
- Are there the right people to lead it? They must have widespread confidence.
- Does it have very clear terms of reference?
- What will be the outcome of its actions? What are the criteria that will give great advantage to telling the truth, and how will that lead towards reconciliation?
- Will it be tied into other parts of the process?

Summary

- Reconciliation is a very long journey. To accomplish anything the travelling must ensure variety of pace, of activity and of content. There must be a mix of milestones with celebrations and steady travelling.
- The structure of a process should be kept as simple as possible. The complexity of the dispute must always be embraced and respected.
- Keep the other Rs going at the same time. The different Rs are cumulative, not successive.
- Ensure that different tracks are used to keep support for the process at all levels, not just the top.

- Use the partnerships required for the job; for example, skilled mediators are specialists.
- Fit the activities to the people, not the people to the activities. But find ways of keeping vision and necessary direction something they reflect on constantly.

Points to Ponder and a Case Study

- Try telling the story of a dispute or conflict from both sides. Do a history backwards exercise; it can take thirty minutes not a day! If not a real one, use the St Thomas case (see p. 118).
- What are good examples of truth being revealed that you know? Whose truth is it? One side? All sides?
- What are the best examples of justice after conflict? How was it done, and does it now seem fair?
- Look for examples of reconciliation you know. Describe the time, the extent and what transformation was needed. What were the key milestones, the moments where things changed? How did they get from one to another? What has been the outcome?
- If there is time, in the working case of St Thomas, ask yourselves how the different groups would imagine a moral and beneficial outcome. What will need to be looked at?

9

Supplies for the Journey – Resourcing

Reconciliation is a process, not an event. Dispute and conflict are addictive drugs. Societies become hooked on them. Research has shown (as mentioned in Chapter 1) that prolonged exposure to conflict literally alters the DNA and has an impact on subsequent generations, especially when the conflict is intergenerational.[1] A group that is always resolving disagreement with destructive forms of confrontation, even when they are violent, can only see solutions in terms of destruction of the other. As the last chapter said, reconciliation is a process of transformation, especially of the moral imagination.

That takes a very long time indeed. The aim is to create habits of dealing with diversity through collaborative endeavour, not simply trying to win. At this point many people will give up and think, 'How naïve!' Sometimes I do myself. Yet history gives us examples of change that demonstrate something far from perfect, but nevertheless offer hope.

Two examples have had a profound impact on the United Kingdom.

The first is the change in Europe since 1945. The European Union may arguably have failed the vision of the founders in some ways but in one respect it has succeeded. France and Germany have not fought each other. North-west Europe has not been a battleground since 1945, the longest period since the fall of the Western Roman Empire. That peace has been achieved by a sustained and deliberate policy of reconciliation and the Franco-German partnership remains the key grouping of the EU 27. For the rest of continental Europe, whether members of the EU or not, that success has altered the way of life. The EU has stabilized democracy in former dictatorships on both sides of the former Iron Curtain. It has helped economies grow rapidly. It has in many ways brought a freedom that is unrivalled in European history. The discussion of what its vision should be now, and whether it can be more than material wealth for some, is for a different place and probably does not include contributions from the UK.

The second is within the UK. From time immemorial the border with Scotland was a place of conflict. The Lords of the Marches, including the Bishops of Durham, had as their first duty the protection of England, and their equivalents north of the border had the task of protection from the English.

The possibility of Scottish independence is very real, something that in other countries might be a cause of war. Yet although the arguments are severe, the reconciliation between Scots and English – except in sport – is so robust that the idea of a war is absurd. Many will find it bizarre even to use that as an example, but for centuries the idea of war being out of any question would itself have seemed utopian in its turn. That is true transformation. Differences remain essential, even encouraged. School systems, the law, Scottish regiments, social policy, the established church, the flag, all differ. We are united but not adversaries, except, as I say, when it comes to sport. Even if the countries divide, it is taken for granted that the process would be by consent, not by war.

Reconciliation happens eventually, even in the most intractable conflict. War-weariness sets in, new leaders appear and what holds people together becomes more important than what causes them to hate. However, we also can point all too easily to conflicts that one can trace back through the ages, whether in the Holy Lands, Afghanistan, parts of Ireland, the Balkans or many other places. Transformation matters. Just because certain types of behaviour are customary and cultural, that does not make them right. Violent solving of disputes should always be a last resort that comes from failure in other approaches, and even then in Christian terms will almost always be wrong.

For example, resorting quickly to violence to resolve disputes is habitual in certain groups, where vendetta is linked closely to honour and shame. Failure to take revenge for an incident in a previous generation brings shame on a family or clan. It is still wrong, but it illustrates the need for transformation and not just peace agreements or a casual hoping that something new may turn up. It is also worth noting that the concepts of honour and shame are very present in all societies, as are vendettas and revenge, even if they are disguised in different clothes.

Very deep transformation is not something done to people by outsiders, but is a heart change, a change of spirit, a change towards an entirely different future. There is nothing new in this dream; in the eighth century BCE the prophet Isaiah wrote of a time when God's rule would come: 'nation shall not lift up sword against nation neither shall they learn war any more'.[2]

In a marriage it can take weeks to recover from a bad argument lasting a few hours. In a community or a church, wounds and disagreements badly handled become part of the folklore and often have very long-term effects. In a nation, or between nations, violent conflict can do damage in a week that takes generations from which to recover. In the UK the legacy of the bitterness of the Brexit campaign of 2016 was still experienced and showed itself in 2021 directly and indirectly, on social media and in political controversy.

The final plate to set spinning is the R of Resourcing the future. No facilitator or group can commit to decades, even generations of involvement, and even if they could it would not in any way be desirable. The presence of outsiders provides opportunities to shift responsibility for a good process to someone else. It creates dependency and it prevents transformation. Those in the conflict need to develop new ways of working, the capacity for moral imagination, the instincts that create possibilities of disagreeing well. They need changed hearts.

It is necessary to recall continually that reconciliation does not seek clones who work together in unanimity. It seeks human beings who grow in diversity and bring all their rich differences together for the common good. The vision of the global Church is that people from every nation should be united in love for Jesus Christ and for their neighbours, meaning in this case, their own locality, as well as further off.

The heart of Jesus' teaching, signs and prayer in John's Gospel is often seen as found in chapter 17. Whole books are written on this passage, which some see as the most profound of the Bible.[3] It is a prayer by Jesus in the minutes before his arrest. In it he prays for his disciples and for those who believe in him because of the testimony of his disciples. The prayer is all-embracing. It begins with prayer for himself, affirming God's authority and his own over the entirety of the creation. It embraces all things and all people, overwhelming every boundary that could exist in the human mind. Jesus prays in this section for the completion of all he is doing as a demonstration of God's glory (vv. 1-5). In the second section he prays for his disciples and their purpose. He prays for their resourcing and for their protection as they carry on the work of Jesus (vv. 6-19). In the last and climactic section (vv. 20-26), Jesus prays for those who will believe through the testimony of his disciples. The theme is the union of all things with God in love, and of the unity of all those who desire God in that unity in love. The vision is breathtaking, impossible to absorb in all its depth and beauty. Described utterly inadequately (who could describe it adequately?), it sees a new humanity abounding in diversity in a world conformed to the love of God and seeking and desiring God with every part of human existence and every last ounce of strength.

In 20.19-23, Jesus comes to the disciples after his resurrection, and in verse 23 he breathes the Holy Spirit of God into them. The Spirit is their equipping to carry on the work of testifying to Jesus, of transforming the world, of cooperating with God in the work of reconciliation of all things.

This sense of the Church (the people of God through time and space) being equipped to become what they are called to be and to carry out the works of God is one that sets a pattern for the whole way in which we treat each other.

It is a vision that is to be a foundation of a new heaven and new earth, where truth, peace and justice reign and all creation rejoices a unity that is made more wonderful by holding together such diversity.

The vision is collective, not individualistic. The prayer and the gift of the Spirit is for all who believe in the name of Jesus, not for all those who believe AND qualify in some other way. God's resourcing is gracious, generous, abundant, overwhelming and transforming. The gift of the Spirit breathes into the receiver the sense of the parenthood of God by adoption. The Holy Spirit creates a new people described in Peter's first letter (2.9-11, NRSV) as 'a chosen race, a royal priesthood, a holy nation, God's own people'. The church is to be a global nation without arms, borders or police, united in love, called by grace, living in peace with all, sent to do the work of God.

This is a vision of complete reconciliation that will take all of human history to reach. It is also a process of equipping those on the journey to travel, to be renewed in their determination and vision and to take responsibility for what they do. God does not give us the option of leaving it all to God in a quietist or fatalistic way, nor does God leave disciples without the necessary means to do the work of being those through whom reconciliation flows to all, and who find the reconciling work of the Holy Spirit already at work.

For facilitators the greatest temptation is to seek the buzz of being needed and to pursue it by moments of high drama and not through the long, undramatic, grassroots work that is of the essence of peacebuilding. For those in senior positions, drama is the way to the possibility of prizes and recognition. Resourcing is about stepping back in a way that enables the journey to go on and grow and deepen in effect and skill and develop its own character, entirely without the presence of the facilitator. Best of all will be when those who are involved in a reconciliation process become peacebuilding facilitators themselves, take the skills they have learned and adapted, and, in their turn, give them away repeatedly.

This process of gift, and the quiet withdrawal, should be almost invisible.

For resourcing to happen, it must be a genuine objective of the facilitators, yet at any level of dispute involving a process of reconciliation, there is a temptation to remain and control, and, with the parties in the dispute, a desire to keep someone else around, if only to blame them for difficulties and to avoid responsibility.

One of the most obvious areas for such dependency is in marital or relationship disputes. Reconciliation can only work when the couple have decided to make it work, when they are clear that they want success in reconciliation, but they may feel that the only safe place for discussion of the most sensitive areas is with a relationship counsellor whom they know. That is fine for a while, but in the end, reconciliation cannot be said to be making serious progress until they are able to handle difficult discussions routinely by themselves.

At the other extreme end of conflict, the presence of UN forces as peacekeepers is both a support and resource, but the sign of serious progress in reconciliation is their withdrawal. In places like the Democratic Republic of the Congo they can become part of the problem if they are there too long.

Reconciliation is a normal part of life. Most people deal with it unconsciously day by day without the slightest need for advice or support. It is made up of apology, of good manners, of letters to clarify and explain, of telephone calls to settle a sense of unease. Sometimes it needs a cup of coffee to clear the air, but mostly we are unaware that we are reconciling; it seems that all we are doing is listening, deepening friendships, helping, hanging out together, sorting things out. It is perhaps over-simplistic, but the list in this paragraph could be called Researching, Relating, Relieving, Risking, Reconciling.

However, when relationships break down seriously between individuals or groups, then we find out whether our relational DNA inclines us towards destructive conflict or towards reconciliation. Where we have grown up and been formed in an aggressive and conflictual style, it is often the case that we lose the capacity to make agreements that work for all, to oil the friction points between groups, to heal hurts and defuse resentments and desires for revenge.

In the days when I was still in the oil industry, I remember one company that appeared incapable of having a discussion without aggression. They were an enormous organization and dominated by a culture that had formed the character of their employees and that went back to the 1920s. On one occasion, I asked someone with whom I had been negotiating why they behaved in such a way. His answer was one of surprise that I had noticed: 'I thought everyone did. It's the way we are trained.' Not only did he behave that way, but he assumed it was the way the world works and should work. The result was that as a company they had more expensive and time-wasting litigation than most of the rest of us combined.

THE COVENTRY WAY

The aim of Resourcing is to begin a culture of reconciliation and leave it with the potential to become the natural way of handling things. That is transformation and it is also transformative for the people involved.

Coventry Cathedral, as I wrote earlier, is a worldwide symbol of reconciliation through the message of its rebuilding, the genius of its architecture and sacred art, and its continuing ministry as a place for training and developing in reconciliation. Yet, like all institutions, it has many ways to have arguments and for people to disagree very strongly with each other – that is because it has human beings attending and participating in its ministry.

Very early in its life after rebuilding, one of the clergy staff sought to address the issue with a structure of groups and of spirituality. That was updated in 2005 as the Coventry Way.[4] It suggests a spirituality of reconciliation based on three concentric circles of relationship, widening out like the ripples of a pond.

Each circle is divided into sub-sections. They are typically about how we learn to deal with different aspects of living in reconciliation, and they vary in each of the three circles.

The **first circle** is about personal spiritual life.

It starts with prayer and scripture. This part is about reconciliation with oneself, the recognition that in Christ we are forgiven, born again and able to begin to live his resurrection life. That involves the hardest reconciliation of all, the acceptance of who one is, the recognition of and repentance and reparation for sins – where possible – and the freedom that comes with the complete forgiveness of

God. It grows in us through our encounter with God in all the intimacy of solitude.

The second part of the first circle is study. Since the time of St Benedict in the sixth century CE it has been understood that Christians need to think long and hard, and to learn from others. For Benedict and the monasteries that obviously involved books and manuscripts; today it will be podcasts, films, TED talks and many other ways of learning and growing in faith through the testimony and understanding of others.

The third part of the first circle is in what the original writers called the Foyer. A foyer in this context is a small group meeting in homes for hospitality, deeper learning and walking together, the practice of extended community, prayer and the study of scripture. These groups must be diverse, for it is unity in diversity that is sought in reconciliation, not unity in identical ideas. The foyers are and should be places of challenge.

The fourth part of the first circle is that of the church congregation, of worship and life together as the body of Christ in a locality or an institution, cathedral, parish, chaplaincy or other local Christian gathering. Relationships will be more distant in any larger church, even of over thirty or so people. Yet this is where it is easy to settle into cliques of the like-minded, identifying most strongly with those with whom one agrees on everything important, even if the most important agreement is one's disagreement with another group. It is important to note that the intimacy and trustful openness of the first two circles is very unlikely to be achieved in a larger group. However, this fourth part is essential for the learning of reconciliation, of love-in-action beyond the natural group of intimates or even of the often hard-earned intimacy of the foyer.

The four parts build on one another. Those who cannot accept that they are loved and forgiven by God (itself a long and progressive journey of reconciliation, but where starting opens the way to transformation), and in that security face the consequences of their sin and deal with it, are unlikely to find it easy or even possible to deal with others in a small group. Those who cannot cross boundaries in a small group will cling to the security of the familiar in the larger circle and exclude others.

The fifth part of the first circle is where the Church reaches out into society through its membership. This will typically mean in the sort of place that Archbishop William Temple described as intermediate institutions.[5] They may be schools, clubs, places of work, almost anything that comes between the central state and the individual or household. The outreach of the Church in such places and institutions is part of normal life. Christians live in retirement homes, or go to work somewhere, or meet others. Here is where the reconciled person who has grown to be a reconciler begins to find themselves encountering disputes and conflict. In the first circle we are called to allow ourselves to be known to be Christians, and in life and love to demonstrate the transforming work of Christ in our lives.

The **second circle** focuses on the way in which a local worshipping community builds up and encourages habits of reconciliation within itself and its life in the world. In this circle the community is called to consider its role in God's world. It is to be a community that is outward-looking locally and globally. It should pray for issues around the world as well as down the street. It should speak and campaign for the common good of its area, and join in the call for justice around the world.

The community should do all these things out of the overflow of the love of Christ, so its own internal reconciliation, worship and prayer life is essential to its lived-out love for those who encounter the community. It will be local as well as global. It is easy to speak clearly about issues over which one has no control and from which there is no fear of retaliation. It will self-audit as to its own standards of justice and listen to its own voiceless, those within its own life who are overlooked and ignored. Depending on the context they may be children and young people, or older people. Often they will be those with a more liberal or more conservative theological, social or political view than the fashion. It may be a group that challenges accepted behaviour and power structures. Essentially, this is where 'love one another' is made real, and it is often very tough. It must pay a living wage to its staff, safeguard the vulnerable and be conscious of exclusions and of imbalances of power.

The local community of worship is the very heart of the work of reconciliation. If it is not active in this way, no one else has the capacity to stand in for it. There is no Plan B.

The **third circle** is about engagement with the world around. From the first circle being the individual, to the second being the worshipping community, the third looks entirely outwards. It is here that a community of reconciled reconcilers, who deal with issues inside their own institution, equip each other to be active in reconciliation wherever their daily lives take them.

Once again, the ministry of reconciliation will start with prayer, but as suggested in Chapter 6 on Relieving, it will develop quickly into the formation of partnerships. Study and research will have revealed local and regional needs, and global prayer and the connections built to pray more knowledgably, through websites and other ways, will mean that different people in the community and in the group of communities that is the wider Church, in partnership with all of goodwill, of all faiths and none, will lead to deep and passionate concern to see transformation in God's world.

One of the greatest examples of such engagement was in South Africa with the fall of the Apartheid regime. The Coventry Cathedral-linked Communities of the Cross of Nails (CCN) were involved, the leadership was interfaith, the basis was seen in the moral standing of President Mandela and Archbishop Desmond Tutu, and all sorts of people around the world were drawn in. The image of the Rainbow Nation grew out of spiritual vision, the avoidance of civil war out of Truth and Reconciliation work, and the outcome continues to be messy, unsatisfactory, but better than it could have been. This is paradigmatic reconciliation work.

It sounds idealized but the examples are numerous. In each of them reconciliation is practised in different ways through the engagement of a worshipping community with areas of need that lead to alienation from society or the embedding of deep structures and powers of injustice and thus division.

Since the financial crash of 2008–09 and the very deep economic recession that followed in the UK, churches have gone into partnership to provide shelter for those sleeping rough. Seven churches will get together during the winter months in order for each one to do so one night a week.

Churches and other groups have also partnered together in providing food banks for those referred to them. Provision is often done through national organizations like the Trussell Trust, which ensures learning and development of best practice.

In many towns and cities, churches have got together to provide night-time patrols on Fridays and Saturday to provide care for those in the night-time scene at clubs and pubs, ensuring their safety, defusing trouble and caring for those who have taken too much of one substance or another. Street Pastors has become a national movement and the police are open and affirming about the reduction in crime and incidents where street pastors are operating.

At a national and international level, reconciliation hubs have set up more local centres to bring groups together, particularly around gang- or militia-controlled areas, and to help broker better ways of life. They have campaigned for nuclear disarmament, as part of protests against economic injustice or racial injustice, and above all in the area of climate change, especially at the major conferences.

At a national level, the Church of England is involved in a project called /together, which seeks, in many different ways, to challenge the deep differences that have grown up in society over the last decade or so. Almost forty different organizations are involved at a variety of points, including polling groups, media, the NHS, and many others. Events may be local or national, but in all cases, they are based around careful research and an effort to reimagine a future with more capacity to disagree well.

The /together project is in many ways the heart of reconciliation and illustrates the model set out in Part II of this book.

It is based on very extensive research, which continues, with large numbers of consultations on the views people of the UK have on what holds society together and where and how serious the divisions are.

It is aimed at deepening relationships at every level from the steering group to the local.

It is based around relieving needs in many ways, especially through existing work of those involved, which covers nearly every aspect of life, and on working in partnerships, avoiding any attempt to reinvent the wheel.

It does not impose views but seeks to take the risk of events and gatherings where relationships are developed, and that may fail.

It is a very long-term process of seeking unity in diversity, of fostering national reconciliation not by overcoming differences of opinion such as Brexit or nationalism, but by changing the way in which disagreements are negotiated.

It is at an early stage of looking at how to resource the way in which we look at difference.

When it comes to the most global of all required reconciliations, of human beings with the natural environment, there is not the time to take generations. Change must happen quickly, certainly by 2030 in terms of policy and some severe action. By 2050 there must be a decisive fall to near net-zero carbon emissions to avoid the climate change that will drive severe and damaging effects on weather generally. Habitability of coastal and of tropical areas in particular will be compromised and will become a driver of many other conflicts as a result of people movements.

The obstacles to the necessary steps are formidable. While most countries admit the problem, the capacity of political elites to lead on a solution appears to be nominal at best. It appears that little will be done if the short-term political cost is high. Here there is a need for internationally approved leadership that can continue not merely to advocate but to advance negotiations at speed. In addition, research needs to continue on necessary costs and a fair balance of burden sharing agreed.

These are uniquely demanding tasks, and it is difficult to see who will lead them. Outside Hollywood films there is no single nation that will save the world, nor is there, rightly, any appetite for such. Countries value their national history and autonomy, often achieved with great struggle. Even if the right leadership can be found, the task of potential mediation is vast. Here we see that the Risking is the point at which there is a danger of the global process being blocked, not by lack of Research, but by inadequate Relating so that love-in-action is missing and thus Risks are too big to contemplate.

The blockage is only resolvable by general political agreement on principles and commitment of political capital now for the generations yet unborn. The prize is a legacy of gratitude for centuries, but much struggle and political cost today.

These conflicts are open to reconciliation, but only with profound commitment politically and a foreswearing of seeking temporary advantage from them. There are many spoilers whose interests are against any reconciliation at all. The mood must change, and that is essentially a grassroots issue. Part III will carry the move from the theory of Part I through the principles of Part II to a grassroots resource for individuals and groups.

Summary

- Resourcing reconciliation means providing the means for those in conflict to be persistent in seeking a way forward.
- In Christian thinking the purpose of God in creating the Church was to have a body that represented and carried on the work of Jesus of reconciliation with God, with creation and with other people.
- The Church and the world are energized and resourced by the gift of God's Holy Spirit, changing hearts, renewing hope, giving strength.
- The divine pattern of reconciliation, as well as a sense of human weakness and forgetfulness of the pain of conflict, leads to the need for deep works of reconciliation to be resourced, perhaps for generations.
- Resourcing involves facilitators being willing to give away their skills, to render themselves superfluous and to fade away, leaving the participants in a conflict who have begun the journey of reconciliation to develop the process in their own way, to add to the skills they have received and themselves to facilitate others.
- For that to happen they must develop a culture, a DNA, of reconciliation. A Christian example, the Coventry Way, is given. Every place, religion, culture will develop its own pattern. At the heart of the Coventry Way are principles of locality, of renewal, of practice in safe settings and of a commitment to going out.

Points to Ponder

- What are your memories of serious and violent conflict like war? Are they first-hand or through friends and relatives? Does it seem to you a distant memory or a recent event?
- How will you pass on to future generations the ideals of peace?
- Within your own circles and organizations or voluntary bodies of which you are a part, do you seek to cross boundaries or stick with those you get on with easily? This is not suggesting that natural friendship groups or common interests are wrong. It is asking where and when – if at all – you form links across boundaries.
- What are the natural boundaries for you? Race or tribe? Age? Social background? Work type and interests? Other things; if so what?
- What are the resources and skills you need to make the effort to form close relationships across natural boundaries?
- Do you know any institution, faith-based or other, that challenges you to make the considerable effort to work at reconciliation?

A Case Study

A couple of years have passed. St Thomas is a better place, the community is stronger but still very fragile. What resources does it need in all the different areas in order to keep going? How can it celebrate progress and the journey still be completed?

PART III

INTRODUCTION

Part I of this book was a meditation on the mystery of reconciliation, asking the question, 'What is it and why is it so difficult to achieve?' Part II looked at a very generalized but practical pattern for approaching issues of reconciliation. This part is the shortest and asks the question, 'What can I do about it?'

The book now seeks to complete the move from the theoretical to the highly practical.

Chapters 10–12 look at the *Difference Course*. *Difference* was first piloted in 2019 and its fifth iteration was published in September 2020. It was designed by the reconciliation team at Lambeth Palace.

The reasons I am focusing on *Difference* are, first, that it has had a very good response in its pilot and beta phases in the UK, South Africa, Hong Kong and the USA. Second, that it is simple, adaptable and down to earth. Third, that it is flexible and accessible. There are many courses of all sorts, but this is the one I know best. I did the course afresh myself, during preparation for writing this book.

Any theoretical structure for reconciliation must answer some questions:

- 'How do I/we start?'
- 'What is a facilitator or reconciler like?'

- 'How do I develop attitudes that make me better at it?'
- 'What difference might this make to me, my household, my group, my church or workplace?'

Difference is a beginning of an answer to those questions.

10

Difference Should Make Us Curious

The *Difference Course* ('the Course', or *Difference*[1]) is designed in its first form for churches. Its aim is enabling people to think for themselves about their attitude to those who are considered by the individual or society at large to be other. As time goes by it will be rolled out in adapted form for secular, other faith and interfaith groups, and in more culturally appropriate ways around the world.

THE REALITY OF THE OTHER

Our capacity to deal with difference is probably no less than it ever was, in many ways it is much better, but the scale of the challenge now appears vast as it is magnified by social media. However, our capacity to do so privately has gone downhill. At a recent Church of England meeting there was discussion about a phrase used by someone in a lecture that could be understood to imply that clergy were unnecessary. People phrase things badly the whole time. I should know as I do it myself. There are a number of rules for dealing with it that used to apply. The first was to ask yourself, 'Did she/he really mean something so bizarre?' and assume the best rather than the worst. The second is that one used to tell the speaker privately what one thought, get it off one's chest and move on. Now people tell the world via social media. Instantly.

There is nothing new about dispute; what is new is the capacity to globalize it. A Convocation (the ancient gathering of clergy and bishops in the Province of either Canterbury or York) in 1689 went on for months, so bitter was the wrangling. But they did not have social media, which was a mercy.

The challenge of dealing with outsiders, or those within the group one belongs to whom one makes outsiders through disagreement, extends around the globe, through much of the natural world, and is not restricted to recent years and issues of racism. It is so much part of being human that for many people it is taken as a virtue, or at least a reality that cannot be challenged. 'They're not like us' is very often a sufficient explanation for antipathy towards incomers.

When I was a parish priest, the wonderful and wonderfully dry-humoured parish clerk said to me once, 'You're not really local until your grandparents are in the churchyard.' I must have looked nonplussed because she went on, 'But you're all right. You may just have arrived as Justin, but as Rector you have been here for 750 years.' It was certainly the way it worked. Dates were sometimes set by reference to when Rector x was here, rather like the time of particular Consuls of the ancient Roman republic were the means of remembering a year.

The point was insiders and outsiders.

On a larger scale, the Church of England has its own gangs. They go by more sophisticated names, such as Evangelical or Traditional Catholic, or Liberal Catholic or Charismatic. There are ways in which one fits into the tribe. Many of these will be very friendly to other tribes, but they are still tribes. One training course run by the Church of England had good reviews, which included the comment from several participants that it was the first time they had worked with Anglicans from a different tradition.

To a large extent such diversity does not do much harm on the surface, and the historic reasons for it is important as well as the fact that each tradition brings value to the Church, but the underlying problem can be a deep sense of competition for control of it. The question often being asked is whether 'they' – whoever they are – obtain more senior appointments and greater control of things. At the extremes it becomes about unchurching people, treating them as outsiders entirely. At that point it becomes even more like political parties and less like the people of God.

Move a step further to political life in the public square and the problem becomes more complicated, and in recent years more damaging. Again, it's an old reality. In *Iolanthe* Act II, a late nineteenth-century comic opera by Gilbert and Sullivan, a sentry on duty during the night at the Houses of Parliament sings,

> I often think it's comical – Fal, lal, la!
> How Nature always does contrive – Fal, lal, la!
> That every boy and every gal
> That's born into the world alive
> Is either a little Liberal
> Or else a little Conservative!

Today we would have to write socialist rather than Liberal, as Labour would not scan, but the reality of the two-party system in England (and the USA) still exists as firmly as ever. Again, the different views are not a problem – but the hatred of one for the other can be.

In 2021 my mother, in her nineties, was admitted to hospital in London. The care she received was wonderful. But when I arrived to see her, she was cross. The excellent Nigerian doctor who had cared for her was told by another patient that she wanted to be seen by an English (i.e. in her mind, White) doctor. Both my mother and I said how sorry and ashamed we were. The doctor took it in his stride. He was highly qualified, patient in attitude, caring in his values. Why would anyone prefer delayed treatment to being treated by him purely on account of his colour? The answer was simply that he was 'other'. If we are easily capable of othering those we see and know – even those we need – how much more easily do we do so for foreigners far away? Asylum seekers, refugees, people in far-off countries of which we know little[2] – all are easily forgotten and ignored.

The list can go on and get broader. Racism, factionalism and other ethnic differences remain among the most pervasive, most deadly and most challenging forms of othering. It may be regions of a country that refuse to let 'settlers' from another part of the same country attend university for both religious and ethnic reasons. In another democracy it may be steps taken to make voting more difficult or to gerrymander constituencies so as to pack all the opposition voters into a smaller number of seats. Either way the othering leads to attacks on human dignity.

It is the slide downwards from recognizing difference to fearing and then hating those who are different that becomes the corrosion that destroys a community or society. The call of Christ is revolutionary in this regard. It is to love God with everything we are. Second, we are then to love one another, those who are 'one of us'. Third, we are to love our neighbours, those with whom we have the common connection of humanity. Fourth, we are to love our enemies.

The revolution goes further than that. We are to love others more than we love our lives. Neighbour is redefined in the Parable of the Good Samaritan (Luke 10.25-37) to be those whose need we see regardless of their otherness. In other words, the Christian community is called to turn away from all hatred. The capacity of Christians to love like this, when it is carried out, is so radical that it reveals the reality that Jesus Christ is God, coming from the Father (John 17.21). The global Church, should it learn so to love amid all the realities of rivalry and distance and desire for power and influence, would turn the world the right way up.

In a book published in 2021, Gordon Brown,[3] the former UK prime minister, discusses global approaches to great problems that threaten large parts of humanity. Reasonably, the first chapter is about the COVID-19 pandemic. He points out that the return to the wealthy countries on money spent to enable a global response to the pandemic is almost US$5 for every dollar spent.[4] In other words, it is an immensely good investment. If someone offered me an investment like that, I would probably turn it down on the grounds it was too good to be true. But it is true. Why then do we not invest as much as we can rather than cutting back on overseas aid? The return would pay the aid budget for years.

The answer is that it is always more difficult to feel a concern for those further away, and that the larger the group of which we speak the more we become consequentialist (what are the outcomes) and even indifferent to moral obligations. The late Rabbi Lord Jonathan Sacks, in his last book, *Morality*,[5] makes this point powerfully. He puts it in a moral context where the moral obligation reaches beyond ourselves and 'home' – as in 'charity begins at ...' – to the common good.

The first step in responsibility for others and thus participation in reconciliation is thus the question of distance, which is effectively where *Difference* starts.

The key response to distance and consequent lack of concern is *curiosity*. Whether it is our neighbour next door who comes from a very different background, the people moving into a new estate on what was the edge of town, immigration pressures or a foreign war, our curiosity is easier to engage nowadays because of good information and it offers a way of shrinking distance.

When encountering those who are other, the most important foundation for overcoming the sense of distance that comes from them being new or different is to listen to their story. The impact of story on who we are is huge. History is not destiny, but it is certainly very influential. The questions about behaviour or attitudes are answered not by seeking to know 'What's wrong with you?', but by the much more open question: 'What is your story; what has happened to you?'

A close relative of ours was a police officer. She was on a call with other officers to deal with a situation of an asylum seeker behaving oddly. He had crawled under a bed and was resisting all attempts to get him out. She lay down so he could see her and asked him about himself, his faith and his history. It turned out later that he had been arrested in his home country and severely tortured by the police there. The sight of police uniforms triggered a reaction. Telling the story enabled the police here to understand and see him as someone who had been a victim of abuse, not a problem.

Being curious brings people nearer as we begin to engage with them in order to understand their concerns and their priorities. Far more than that, it puts them in the category of those whose good we seek.

In the Old Testament in the Book of the Exodus, the Israelites are settled in Egypt where they have been for generations. Having originally gone down from Canaan in order to avoid a famine, they had been welcomed and settled through the agency of Joseph, who ruled Egypt for the then Pharaoh. Exodus 1.8 starts a new part of the story, saying: 'Now a new king arose over Egypt, who did not know Joseph.' The Pharaoh looks at the strength and numbers and prosperity of the people of Israel and sees them as a threat. To be ignorant of a person or a group is to leave space for fear. In some cases, knowledge may justify fear, but in almost all circumstances it reduces it and makes space for reconciliation.

The result of the ignorance of Pharaoh is, first, oppression of the Israelites, the long-standing descendants of economic immigrants; second, their ill-treatment; and third, outright war against both them and God. Ignorance settles us into hostility.

Exodus is the story of the liberation of God's people by God's supreme power. Reading other texts alongside Exodus, Egypt becomes the symbol of several aspects of Israelite existence. It is the place of slavery. It is the place of refuge, as with Jesus himself as an infant. It is a place of betrayal, a hope for Israel when oppressed by others, but a hope that always fails, as with the exile when Egypt's help is sought against Babylon, but Egypt does not deliver. Egypt contrasts with God, who is trustworthy and faithful, the place to turn for help. Finally, however, Egypt, like every other nation, will be called faithfully to turn to God in repentance and obedience.

All these stories are the stories of Israel. They define who they are, and thus how they are known, by the stories they tell about themselves. To keep them faithful they recount the story of the Exodus at the Passover. They are to teach their children, who are to be curious. In being curious they will meet the greatest 'other' that exists, God, and in knowing the story of God with God's people they will hear the call to turn to God and be faithful.

The greatest reconciliation is between human beings and God. God is revealed in God's story, through the life of Jesus Christ. Being curious is not just a means of overcoming ignorance and thus fear; it is the means of discovering the depths of love that are possible across difference.

The *Difference Course* applies the habit of being curious in five sessions, as with the other two habits of being present and reimagining.

The first session is about God's command to be peacebuilders and reconcilers. How does our being curious show itself overall in our ways of living? Where do we get information from? Is it only one source or does it include those with whom we disagree?

I listen to podcasts and read publications that make me feel good because they agree with me and say that what I am doing is right – well, I have never found one of those, but one day, somewhere? – but I also read things or listen to podcasts that keep my blood pressure up, at least metaphorically. I look for intelligent criticism, out of curiosity about the views that I do not currently accept. Over time some of them change my views. I also try to mix with a variety of people who have very different views and to listen carefully.

We are all aware that the tendency of social media is to draw us into bubbles of the like-minded. Many people will know the somewhat illicit satisfaction emotionally that comes from hearing a good speaker telling them how right they are and how wrong their opponents are. Its known as preaching to the choir.

One of the most striking features of the debates around sex and gender and transgender is that, according to some, to disagree is not only to be wrong, but to be evil. Similarly, the questions about the levels of racism in the UK institutionally lead not merely to very robust debate, but to death threats and profound abuse of the individuals concerned.

The stirring-up effect of social media is critical in this area. Try doing an audit of those you follow on social media, of the podcasts to which you listen, of those you follow on Instagram, TikTok and all the other forms of media that spring up and die down. What proportion are those with whom you disagree?

The second session of *Differences* is called 'Crossing Divides'. There are, speaking as a clergyman, certain ways of encouraging a congregation to take a Sunday off church. One is to announce that you are going to preach on giving. Another is to share a service with a different church, or to do a pulpit swap. There is nothing malicious about people being away; they like what they know, the familiar.

In John 4.1-30 we read how Jesus met and talked with a Samaritan woman at a well in Samaria. That encounter shocked his followers as he crossed gender and ethnic boundaries. He demonstrated the spiritual insights of curiosity-in-loving-action, which is far different from nosiness. It was a curiosity that spoke to her of hope and a future, of a better life than she had known and of one that could be lived by her whole village. Yet the first step for Jesus was to ask for a drink of water.

Where are the places that offer the chance to cross boundaries? It may be a local meeting of the Council of Christians and Jews. It could be visiting another church. A friend in the USA was aware of Dr Martin Luther King saying that Sunday morning is the most segregated two hours of the week in America because Christians all go to churches full of people like themselves. He therefore visited all the churches in his part of Virginia, of all denominations and all ethnicities. At the Black Pentecostal churches, he was very warmly welcomed. His own church was Episcopalian and very White. He tried, mostly unsuccessfully, to get the ministers to visit other churches, and then members of the congregations. Yet they all felt it would not be safe, and that they preferred to be where they had always been, not hating each other but not in unity-within-diversity either.

We are commanded to cross divides because you cannot build bridges without being on both sides of a divide. We are commanded to be boundary breakers, because you cannot bring reconciliation without crossing boundaries.

The third session is on disagreeing well. 'Disagreeing well' is a controversial phrase. Shortly after I used it for the first time (I have no doubt it does not come from me in the first place, but I picked it up somewhere), I was firmly criticized on the grounds that Christians should not disagree. To which my answer is, 'But they do! Incessantly! And who says they should not?'

Paul is always dealing with disagreements in churches to which he was writing; look at 1 Corinthians 1, Romans 12-15, and the stories about Paul personally (e.g. Acts of the Apostles 15.36-41, but cf. 2 Timothy 4.11). He tells the church to be of one mind or to have the same mind in Philippians 2.2, but the context is to avoid destructive divisions of jealousy and anger.

Disagreeing well requires being curious about the real thinking of the person with whom you disagree. Instead of trolling, or cutting off contact, or ignoring and effectively cancelling, it is worth asking, 'Please would you explain your reasons for what you think?'

The fourth session concerns practising forgiveness. All Christians are called to be forgiven forgivers, reconciled reconcilers. In the way that a doctor practises in their identity as a doctor so should we practise in our identity as forgiven forgivers. At the same time, we are generally very bad at it and thus practice is important in every part of life.

One of the schools that our children attended taught the very small pupils to say sorry when they had fallen out and then for the wronged one to say, 'I forgive you.' It spread, with some difficulty, into our family. Forgiveness is harder to give and receive than apologizing, saying sorry.

Sorry is a powerful weapon of passive aggression. It is also a well-established way of conceding with a non-concession. In a satirical political sketch, one of the leading politicians says words to the effect of, 'If you feel offended by my accusing you of fraud and treason, then I am sorry.' A genuine apology would be: 'I accused you of fraud and treason, I was wrong. Please forgive me.' Yet the 'non-apology apology' is the most frequently used. Anything that begins with 'if' and puts the blame for being offended on the victim is a non-apology. Anything that leaves the more vulnerable trapped into being manipulated towards forgiveness is not an apology.

Forgiveness is one of the toughest parts of reconciliation. It is often manipulated and usually misunderstood.

The manipulation comes, as I have said, through putting the pressure on the victim. For example, with regard to the need for racial and ethnic reconciliation in the UK there is often the explicit or implicit suggestion that Black people should forgive so that we can all move on. In the safeguarding of children and vulnerable adults, perpetrators have piled abuse upon abuse by requiring forgiveness or by using sacraments such as the confessional and saying that the victim/survivor is required to keep it secret. In a recent case the survivor was told that the perpetrator had sought the forgiveness of God and therefore the survivor must treat it as past. That is a blasphemous misuse of forgiveness by the perpetrator.

In these and many other ways the notion of forgiveness is distorted and the most precious of gifts, the greatest treasure, is soiled in the hands of the manipulators.

God calls us to be forgiven forgivers. Forgiveness is, however, not the same as forgetting the consequences. We can forgive someone who still is sent to prison for a crime against us. The indescribably awful national sins committed through slavery, through Empire and in war, by many nations, may by grace and goodness be forgiven by those who are the descendants of the victims and whose lives are still affected by what happened, directly and indirectly. Yet the offer of forgiveness is not the same as waiving justice. It will still be necessary to show repentance and make reparation, not to earn forgiveness but as a real sign of a change of heart. As I wrote earlier, actions, even of those long before us, have consequences. That is part of what the great Conservative political philosopher Edmund Burke[6] meant by his speaking of the social contract as a covenant with those who have lived, those who are alive today and those who are yet to be born.

To be curious opens the way to practise forgiveness. It is to enquire into the state of mind of a perpetrator, to seek to understand their thinking, to sense their guilt and desire for change. It is also to understand one's own feelings. I know the desire, when I have suffered wrongly, for the perpetrator to be made to regret deeply how wrongly they have acted. I wanted them to feel what I felt. It took time to set that aside, to battle with God in prayer in order to see my anger and to find his love. Psalm 137 speaks of the Jewish exiles in Babylon cursing their captors who saw them as entertainment: the exiles wanted their enslavers to see their own children murdered as they had murdered the children of Jerusalem. I have sat with Christian leaders in the ruins of their town by the mass graves of their families listening to them speak of their inescapable pain and desire for revenge.

The Quentin Tarantino film *Django Unchained* (2012) is a revenge story, full of blood and violence. Although the escaped slave Django kills many, one cannot help but empathize with his anger at the cruelty of his White oppressors. To be curious is not to reject justice. To be curious must mean that one seeks to enter the feelings of those who suffer and those who oppress, while also seeking justice. Archbishop Desmond Tutu was a passionate advocate of the oppressed, but sought to love their oppressors so that they might see their wrongdoing. He was never neutral between perpetrator and victim, but neither was he consumed with a desire for revenge.

Forgiveness frees the victim from the chains of hatred. It enables the victim to seek justice and campaign for righteousness. It is a liberation, it is a gift to us from God, but it is never a tool with which to oppress further the already oppressed, the abused, the weak and the vulnerable. It is a key to freedom, not a club for the powerful to impose settlement.

The final session of *Difference* is about hope. It is called 'Risking Hope' because it sets hope clearly in the context of offers made and expectations arrived at, but with the risk of neither being fulfilled.

As the epistle to the Romans says in 5.5: 'hope does not disappoint us because God's love has been poured into our hearts through the Holy Spirit that has been given to us'. The *Difference Course* says: 'we need to know that we are called to be part of God's story of restoration in the world'.[7] In C. S. Lewis's book *The Great Divorce*, hell is full of those without hope and with regrets, and heaven is a place of ever-growing joy in an ever-greater place, journeying together in forgiveness and hope to an ultimate destination. The journey begins in pain, with the reality of heaven making even grass as sharp as glass, but eases as progress is made. Lewis paints a similar picture in the final part of his Narnia Chronicles, *The Last Battle*.

Hope is, however, often unexpressed and in short supply. To be curious is to ask yourself about your own hopes and to ask your community about theirs. The curiosity will be fed by the act of crossing boundaries, of practising forgiveness, of disagreeing well. All these build community and communities are built to grow on hope. Churchill's speeches in 1940 were great for many reasons, but chief among them was that they gave hope. His capacity for great errors was huge, but his capacity for inspiring hope was even greater. In any community, reconciliation will be strengthened by hope, but hope must be made known, declared and owned.

SUMMARY

- The first of the key habits of reconciliation is curiosity, being curious.
- We need a lively but not busybody curiosity in order to build bridges and cross divides, so as to understand the stories of others.
- We need a curiosity that listens carefully to those with whom we disagree so that we may disagree well and be able to tell their story and put their argument as well as we can our own, even when we disagree.
- Being curious about our own feelings and the reality of the motivations of others will enable us to practise the hard work of forgiveness. Forgiveness is not the same as allowing injustice.
- We need to be curious about our own and others' hopes, so that in community we may grow in faith and love.

Points to ponder are to be found in the *Difference* resource and website.[8] The only one I will mention now is whether you know of a group that would like to try the *Difference Course* together.

11

Being Present

The temptation to save time by multi-tasking is hard to resist normally. Why not have the mobile on the kitchen table during family meals? Why not do emails during some kinds of conversation? When there is a telephone conference call, or even a video conference, if my laptop is below the camera's reach, do something else as well, it saves time later. And it's not only multi-tasking. Politicians in long and doubtless boring meetings are regularly caught playing games on a smart phone, or texting or using social media.

Yes, but ... It tells everyone that you are *not present*. It tells the family that the caller at a meal is more important than they are. It tells people they do not have your attention. Above all, it means that you are not listening properly, engaging creatively, exercising the double hearing of listening to the people you are meeting and to the Spirit of God. Love-in-action means being present, and being present is the second of the habits of the *Difference Course*.

It begins with theology. We should be present to others as a commitment of love because God was, is and always will be present as a commitment of love to us.

God sees and knows everything. The consistent celebration of the Psalms is that God sees, except in a very few psalms of lament and protest where the psalmist calls for him to look. That theme of lament and protest is also picked up in many modern theologians of the Global South. It is a theological theme that emerges from suffering and injustice. Yet the presence of God in the Old Testament and the New is seen as deeply dangerous. Where God is visible it is either in a form of possible incognito (as with Abraham before the condemnation of the cities of the plain, Genesis 18) or as a cause of fear (with Gideon, Judges 6.22; the calming of the storm in the New Testament; the announcement of the birth of Jesus to the shepherds; and many other places). God's presence is so awesome that it may lead to death. In the New Testament the coming of Jesus is God's presence in a way foretold through the Old Testament but drawing into God all that is human by taking on the form of a servant, fully human, and in that extraordinary mystery suffering with all human beings. Presence in the incarnation is presence to everything in life, and to death.

In John 14.16, Jesus promises his disciples that he will send the Holy Spirit to be present – a promise fulfilled after the resurrection – and to this day, in the gift of the Spirit of God, to make all alive in Christ and to carry on the creative and sustaining work of God in all the world and all of creation.

The Church – in the sense not of the institution but of the people who are Christians – makes many mistakes about the presence of God through the Spirit.

Too often we try and confine the Spirit to God's areas of work as *we* see them, as if God had a job description and we had to monitor it properly. At worst there is in

some churches and traditions the sense that though God
may be at work everywhere, God is especially at work in
'our congregation' or 'our church or denomination'. It
will seldom be put like that, although I have heard it, but
it is often implicit in the way certain groups speak. It is
often a tool of control by manipulative church leaders, or
a sign of a deep arrogance.

Slightly less bad, but still an implied caging of God
the Spirit, is the sense that God is only at work in the
Church universal and not outside it. There is a feeling
that God would not want to be contaminated by dealing
with people who are not like God, as if God did not
have enough practice. It reveals itself in pietism, where
involvement with the things of the world around us is
wrong. It sees areas like reconciliation as only the real deal
when they involve the Church. I remember being asked
when I worked at Coventry Cathedral why I bothered
with reconciliation involving people who were not
Christians? Should I not be preaching the gospel to them?
My answer now would be that I was preaching the gospel
and that I worked in those circumstances and places, and
still do, because when I get there I find God at work, and
I join in to learn.

To put it less informally, the creative and sustaining
work of God is revealed in Jesus Christ, the Prince of
Peace. In Colossians 1.15-20 St Paul speaks of the cosmic
Christ in whom 'all things hold together' (17, NRSV) and
'through Him God was pleased to reconcile all things,
whether on earth or in heaven, by making peace through
the blood of his cross' (20, NRSV). 'Everything', 'all
things', the piling up of words indicates Paul's passionate
proclamation of the truth of Christ. The human ministry
of peacemaking is, consciously or unconsciously, worked

out in the day to day, by human beings imperfectly and partly, seeking the glorious reconciliation of all things that is the purpose of God.

The presence of the peacemaking Christ is thus always and everywhere. The pleasure of God in reconciling all things (as in Colossians) is in a cosmic reconciliation, of all of creation, for God is the Creator. It is not just with human beings, or even this planet. Those who are involved in peacemaking, who are seeking or supporting reconciliation, have therefore to be present because God is present. Being present, as I admitted in starting this chapter, is often difficult.

As with being curious, the five sessions of *Difference* each have some thinking and challenge on the habit of being present.

GOD'S CALL

When I was training for ordination, I had a work placement with the chaplain of the local hospital. His main feedback was that I needed to learn to be more present with those I was visiting. I did not like hospitals. I was unsure of my role and found the process difficult, and it showed. He was quite right, and the lesson stuck in my mind. During the COVID-19 pandemic, during 2020 and 2021 I have had the privilege of supporting the superb senior chaplain at Guy's and St Thomas' Trust in London. This involved regular time spent in the hospital, with the critically ill in COVID-19 wards or others. I have tried to put the lesson of those many years ago into practice in this recent experience.

We all have encounters we do not like. For many people they involve confrontation, or difficult conversations.

Most of us will be familiar with the sinking feeling of waking in the morning, thinking through the day, and knowing that there will be an event or a meeting that we dread. It may not happen often, but we avoid it.

It is always easier to be with people you like and get on with naturally. One of the lessons that both my wife Caroline and I have had to learn in my role as Archbishop of Canterbury is how to work a room. That is, when there is a reception or gathering, to ensure that time is spent with everybody. It is a discipline because you always come across people with whom you want to chat. They may be old friends, and it is just easier. They may be complete strangers, but utterly fascinating.

Being present is a habit. It needs self-awareness like all habits. God's call is to be present across the range of people, to be not only present but a presence that people know and trust. *Difference* encourages us all to see who we choose not to mix with; how we use the opportunities to be present.

It is worth breaking down your time into those different aspects of life, like leisure, work, family, church, friends. You may be part of a club or sports group of some kind, or of an association that does things together. Who is avoided and who is easy to be with?

How we are present can be a very important sign of the health of significant relationships. Sometimes people will spend more time at the office or more time outside the home because their marriage is difficult. An audit of what we do and what we avoid doing will show us where the lights are flashing a warning. Absence is often not a way of making the heart grow fonder but of avoiding the reality of a heart that has grown less fond. Reconciliation requires being present.

CROSSING DIVIDES

Every year there is a service in a cathedral or major church for police officers who have died in service, whether in the line of duty or any other reason. The service rotates around the different nations and regions of the UK. One year it was at Liverpool Cathedral and the Prince of Wales attended, as he always does. After the service there was a reception for him with the families of officers who had died within twelve months. There were around a hundred and twenty present, with the most recently bereaved having lost a partner about three weeks earlier.

It was a deeply moving occasion. I was struck that the Prince was 'present' to each family he met as if they were the only ones there. I learned a great deal just watching. The impact of his interest, focus and compassion was healing for all.

It was not just because he is the Prince of Wales, although that was very significant. Added to that was the way in which he engaged. Being present is much more than physical. It means engaging the whole of oneself.

As was written earlier, 'remember the body'. In a hospital, where it is appropriate for the person, touch, holding a hand, matters greatly. The body's sense of touch is very significant both positively and negatively. Some people dislike personal space being invaded in that way, some who are isolated find it comforting and full of meaning.

Eyes are important. A person at St Thomas' was gravely ill in critical care. I remember above all their eyes. They had COVID-19, could not speak, were exhausted and quite possibly not far from the end of their life. But their eyes held mine and spoke volumes. Not only in those very extreme circumstances or those of someone bereaved, but also in mediation, the engagement of look and attention is significant of presence.

Of course, everything needs calibrating. When we meet someone for the first time, normally we do not want a deeply intense encounter. There are people I have met who fix me with their eyes and say, 'How are you really?' My normal answer is 'Fine, thank you', although sometimes I want to say (but never do), 'That's my affair.'

Being present can be just as simple as showing up. Look around at your neighbourhood, at other churches, at different religious communities. Find out what can be done together by going to be with them. Go to places and meet people you normally are distant from. Cross boundaries.

DISAGREEING WELL

Being present when bored in long meetings requires discipline. Being present when having a disagreement is another thing altogether; it requires courage.

There are many ways in which we seek to avoid being present in such circumstances. One is to be physically absent. I am aware of one colleague with whom I worked who always had a reason for being somewhere else when it was clear that there was going to be disagreement. It was always polite, always reasonable, and always happened. The result was too often that the can got kicked down the road and the disagreement, when it was properly faced, was much more difficult to deal with and often led to disagreeing badly.

The skills of facilitators and of mediators – they are not exactly the same thing – have an overlap in that they involve enabling those disagreeing to be present to each other and for the deepest reasons for the disagreement to be faced. As a result of these skills, the use of facilitation and mediation is growing so that some organizations almost never have a meeting without an outside leader.

That in its turn leads to another way of not being present: hiding behind the process of disagreeing well. To be truly present means to develop the skills of disagreeing and to do so without being defensive. We are all aware of having heard defensive answers to interviewers on current affairs programmes. A public figure leading an organization has acted badly themselves or the organization for which they are responsible has done so. Their answers to probing questions begin with explanation or with a negative. 'You don't understand' or similar phrases abound.

It is the same in disagreeing. We may be present physically, we may be curious, but our presence needs to be undefended. We are truly present when we listen and reflect on what is being said, when we enquire (being curious) to understand better.

It is a severe test. No one likes to say that they are wrong. Yet we will not disagree well unless the whole of us, including our vulnerabilities, is present.

Practising Forgiveness

My own experience of forgiveness, forgiving and being forgiven is mixed and human. A severe wound from someone almost always leads to a desire to be away from them. The nature of relationship breakdown – whether with a friend, a lover, a spouse, child or parent – is above all one of absence. In my own childhood, like so many children I had the experience of a family where parents were not together and there was, in one household, much anger. The means of dealing with that complicated relationship as very much the weaker party was to withdraw emotionally, even when present.

So many of us do that. Cut our losses, sever the relationship, don't speak about the person any more.

Yet that understandable way of dealing with emotional pain as a child needs to be grown out of if we are to become whole adults. Forgiveness is a necessity for a functional society, however much it is a challenge for individuals. We must recognize – I have already discussed this but it bears repetition – that when encountering one person or a group that have been the victims of cruelty, sometimes on a vast scale, the imposition of an obligation to forgive can easily become more abuse.

Yet at a societal level there needs to be institutional presence. The habit for the powerful of being present to those who have suffered from their power is one essential component of developing into a society that is capable of forgiveness. The importance of being present and risking pain is an essential to arrive at a place that is honest about forgiveness and that gets past manipulation. Even more powerful is the presence of those who have suffered, who are so often not asked for permission for the powerful to be there, or the terms on which the powerful are there.

That sort of institutional presence is a severely endangered species. Presence may be very rare, for example, between police and groups like young Black people that want to challenge with a sense of victimization or between different groups who hold clashing views on the nature of the rights of transgender people. The lack of presence may be fear of confrontation, often based on past experience; it may even be the arrogance of power. Whatever the causes of not wanting to be present, those meetings, if presence is genuine, will have to take the chance of including space to ask for and to offer forgiveness for past wrongs. The alternative to presence is to remain in trenches lobbing social media grenades at each other to little or no effect.

RISKING HOPE

Being present is a huge risk. To be present implies hope, above all hope that progress can be made amid difficulty in relationships or in conflict. In Part II, Chapter 7 looked in some depth at the whole issue of risk, and especially the risks involved in meeting. To take those risks and then be physically but not properly present is a certain route to failure.

Yet to be present feels like betting everything on a very uncertain outcome. In John's Gospel, chapter 6, Jesus – among many other things – deals with being present. In the chapter there are two miracles, or signs in John's language: the feeding of the five thousand and walking on water. Jesus makes himself present to the crowd when the disciples want to avoid presence by sending them away to get food. He then absents himself from the crowd and his disciples when they seek to use their numbers to make him a king. Instead of being with them, he, like Moses on Sinai, goes up a mountain and is present with his Father, God. He comes to the disciples on the waters of the windy lake and remains with them (a key concept in John is remaining, staying). The crowd are seeking him, another key word, linked to presence. When he challenges them as to what they seek – are they genuinely present to him because he is the bread of life, or only as a high-value grocer with miraculous logistics? – they leave.

They will not be present on Jesus' terms but only on their own. Presence goes with curiosity, and as we will see, with reimagination. The crowd's presence is quite unlike that of Jesus' disciples. The crowd know what they want, and will only be present for what they want. Presence in that way avoids the risks of disappointment. It is not making oneself vulnerable, which true presence does.

Then Jesus turns to his disciples and asks them (vv. 67-69, NRSV): "'Do you also wish to go away?" Simon Peter answered him, "Lord, to whom can we go? You have the words of eternal life. We have come to believe and know that you are the Holy One of God."'

Jesus is challenging them to be present. Peter's response is to say, plaintively, that in Jesus is hope. They must be present with him because that is the risk to be taken for that hope to be fulfilled. They do not know what is going on, but they know that in Jesus is hope. In that way their presence is genuine; it commits to mutual relationships amid the fog of not knowing.

SUMMARY

- Being present is an obvious habit to develop because no relationship can be built without it.
- To be genuinely present, especially with those with whom we disagree, is very difficult. We long to run away from the challenge.
- Being present at a shallow level is insufficient to build unity in diversity.
- Being present is something that happens with groups and institutions as well as individuals. It enables systemic reconciliation.

- The culture of avoiding those with whom we disagree is one that leads to more and more fracturing and less and less of an abundant life for everyone.
- Jesus was not afraid of being present, including to God. To be hopeful requires us to be present at greater depth, especially when our hope is in God.

Points to Ponder

- In prayer are you present to God entirely, or only those bits of you that you think God will like?
- Are there a few simple rules you can set for yourself to be more present to family, friends and work colleagues or others? How does your use of electronic gadgets affect you being present?
- Are there people from whom you have drifted? What are the options to renew a mutual presence?
- Are you good or bad at difficult conversations? Can you decide to have them AND decide not to be defensive but to be present?

12

Reimagining

As we all know, the imagination works in bizarre ways. What we imagine in our sleep, as dreams, is wildly beyond anything we could imagine while awake. Some people have a disciplined, practical but unimaginative approach to challenges. Others have flights of fancy that are amazing but lack all capacity to turn them into reality. In most areas of life there are the occasional geniuses whose imaginations enable them to forge new directions in hopeless situations or new ideas in a time without ideas, and who also have the knowledge, skills and discipline to make it happen.

Examples abound throughout history. In recent times we can think of Captain Sullenberger landing a crippled aircraft on the Hudson River in New York without losing a single life. He had no engines, no height and no space, but he both imagined and performed the landing. We can think of J. K. Rowling imagining a world with witches and wizards who hide in plain sight and writing seven volumes of coherent narrative that grips people of every age and contains a profound morality. She imagined, but then she wrote something that makes sense in its own terms. We can think of Václav Havel, a political prisoner of the communist government of Czechoslovakia, or Nelson Mandela of South Africa, prisoner of the Apartheid regime, imagining freedom, gaining freedom without a collapse into civil war and then building a nation on a basis of seeking reconciliation. Of course, things went wrong, but skill and imagination kept them on course as long as they were alive.

The list is endless. We can list names like St Hildegard of Bingen correcting and challenging emperors in the Europe of the Middle Ages, Elizabeth I, Jane Austen, Florence Nightingale, Churchill, or Washington, or Augustine of Hippo. It goes back to Homer, Dido, Cleopatra, Aristotle. Athletes like Jesse Owens at the 1936 Olympics, Lewis Hamilton in motorsport, Emma Raducanu at the 2021 US Tennis Open, are all a mix of ambition, determination, imagination, and skill forged in practice.

We are used in music, the arts, sport, politics, and every area of human endeavour to the idea of imagination. It is an indispensable part of success and nowhere more than in situations where conflict and disagreement have reduced hope and eliminated expectations of a better world. It is one thing to be imaginative when all is going well. It is quite another to be able to reimagine a future that is different and to develop the tools for bringing it into reality.

One of the supreme examples of imagination is the famous speech of Dr Martin Luther King Jr on 28 August 1963, at the Lincoln Memorial in Washington, to a vast crowd who had marched for civil rights. One of the most often-quoted parts is: 'I have a dream that my four little children will one day live in a nation where they will not be judged by the color of their skin, but by the content of their character. I have a dream today!' Not only was it rhetoric of an extraordinary skill but it gave a crowd and a nation, weighed down by racial division and oppression, a vivid idea of possibilities that they themselves had not imagined. It put deep hopes into tangible form, something to aim for, a vision not only for dreams, but also for practical ambitions. Even unknown people may, by an act of courageous reimagination, change the course of events. Seven years before Dr King's speech, Rosa Parks, in Montgomery, Alabama, refused to give up her bus seat for a White man. It was a major step in the struggle towards justice and civil rights.

Imagination is not a one-off moment after which the serious work begins. It is a process that is twinned with the use of skills and that leads to reimagination as progress is made or as setbacks occur and new ways forward need to be found.

In November 2012, the General Synod of the Church of England (a sort of church parliament) declined to support proposals that would have permitted the ordination of women as bishops. The mood in the days after the vote was very dour. The approach that would make it possible had been thrashed out over a great many years, decades even, and endless reports and periods of prayer and deep theological reflection. There was contempt for the failed process expressed in Parliament and in many newspapers. The general opinion was that it would be five years before another attempt could be possible.

However, in the immediate aftermath of the vote a group of people, both women and men, began to reimagine the possibilities of a different way forward. Much hard work was done on the legal detail and many conversations took

place between people of differing views. To cut a very long
story short, in July 2014 a simpler form of the legislation
was passed and the first woman to be nominated a bishop
was announced before the year end, a bare two years after
the failed vote.

That was an example of reimagination, along the lines
of 'if this does not work, but its failure had an impact,
let's try a new approach, building on the new mood'.
Reimagination has to happen again and again and that
is why it is the third of the habits that the *Difference
Course* seeks to inculcate. It links, obviously, to Lederach's
moral imagination, discussed in Part I.[1] It is more than a
practice, or a discipline, it has to be a habit. Imagination
is not always spontaneous; in my case, very seldom. My
default is to plod on. The habit of reimagination needs
to grow to the point that it is always there, as part of the
character of the group, or nation, or individuals.

The Bible is full of reimagination that opens the
way forward to new developments and finds a way to
deal with potential serious conflict. In the Acts of the
Apostles 10.1-11.18 (Acts) there is one of the most
significant reimaginings of the call and purpose of God
for the people of this world. From very early in his public
ministry, Jesus encountered Gentiles who were seeking
help or advice. Earlier in this book we looked at the story
of the Syrophoenician woman whose child was possessed
by a demon. Jesus challenges her as to his mission but her
answer in faith leads him to act. There are many other
examples of boundary crossing, both by Jesus and by the
apostles after his ascension. In Acts chapters 10 and 11
and thereafter the mission of the Church is pushed by
the Holy Spirit of God into taking a decisive turn to the
Gentile world.

As a result, over the following decades Gentiles of a huge variety of backgrounds and cultures became the dominant groups among Christians. The first reaction of Jewish believers was shock. In Acts 11.1-18 Peter tells believers in Jerusalem the story of his encounter with a Roman centurion (the events are recorded in Acts 10), after Peter had seen a vision, and of the centurion and his household receiving the Holy Spirit in the same way as the Jewish believers. From there the Gentile mission spreads to Antioch, through Asia Minor, to Greece and to Rome and beyond. It is the moment at which Christianity turned from being a Jewish group to a potential worldwide religion.

Throughout Christian history the response to radical change in circumstances has been a process of reimagining theologically the mission and actions of the global Church. With the fall of the western Roman Empire in the fifth century CE, Augustine of Hippo rethought the shape of a church in a western world without a centralized and powerful empire, but a Church surrounded by anarchy. In Ireland, northern England and Scotland, long before Augustine of Canterbury came in 597 CE, Celtic missionaries reshaped the way the Church worked, with few or no bishops and with bases in monastic communities. At times of great decline and division in the Church, figures like St Francis of Assisi, St Benedict and St Teresa of Ávila have emerged with a reimagining of the transformation and reconciliation of the gospel. Where the institution was willing to be inspired by reimagination, the Church found purpose and renewal, was reconciled to God and to each other, and recovered a missionary zeal and a commitment to Christ. Where they refused, most notably for all sides in the Reformation, division occurred.

Reimagining is the means of retaining a vision when circumstances have altered.[2] The events in Acts 10 and 11 were in the context of growing persecution, the murder of some of the Christians in the Holy Land and the scattering of believers all over the Roman world. Reimagining is both collective and individual but is usually much more effective in a group. It is not the unthinking acceptance of a new direction, but, as in the passage from Acts, a carefully tested and examined set of proposals that seems good to the consensus of those concerned.

God's Call

The source of all good imagination, of vision and of hope, is God. The test of genuine reimagining is that it reflects the love of God revealed in Jesus Christ and testified to by the Bible. The limits of reimagining the extent of reconciliation are the limits of God, which is another way of saying that there are no limits. When we combine the work of God through Jesus Christ in reconciliation, we find that the call to be peacebuilders is a call to imitate God. It is not the work of specialists and technical experts. It is a call to the whole Church of God, every Christian person, and on every occasion on which each of us falls short of that call we fall into sin. Yet God knows our weakness. My own experience is of constant falling and failure, but also of the love of God who picks me up and gives me a fresh start. That is the constant tension all Christians live with.

Holiness is seen in many ways. For the wounded and oppressed it may be simply that they call out to God. Paul speaks to slaves in his letters, telling them just to try to work well. So does Peter in his first letter. God knows us,

our sufferings, our weakness and our failures. To go back
to my friend Désiré in eastern Congo, 'Do what we can' –
the rest is God's problem.

At a global level, holiness calls us to seek to reconcile
the creation with human existence, even if the cost is
very great, and our contribution very small. The creation
is not ours; it is God's. We are the stewards and our
reconciliation with creation, including climate and
biodiversity, is also an essential part of holy living in
reconciliation with God.

At a global, national and community level, the
reconciliation of race and ethnicity, as well as class, gender
and sexuality, nationality and other differences, is a holy
call. It does not mean that everything wanted by everyone
is right, but that finding out what is right depends on
a foundation of living in a reconciled disagreement that
enables us to search for the will of God. We cannot live
in holiness and hatred, or holiness and enmity. They are
incompatible.

As a global Church we must not rest comfortably
among our divisions and rivalries. Ecumenism grew up in
the 1920s out of a desire for unity. That unity must be our
constant desire and to the extent that it is not yet possible
to find a common voice of unity institutionally we must
do so by cooperation through love-in-action.

As a global Church we must seek to find ways of relating
well to other faiths. Christians have always lived among
other faiths, but have too often been tyrannical when in
the majority. The intense need for interfaith engagement
becomes stronger as the proportion of the world's
population in one faith or another grows and as faith
becomes, in many countries, more and more a tool of
politicians to define who is 'us' and who are our enemies.

God's call is shown by God's example in Jesus, who gave up heaven to become poor in this world for our sakes, to die for our sakes, for our sakes to rise and for our sakes to give the Holy Spirit so that a new body may emerge that crosses every boundary and exists in love and freedom and light in a dark world.

At the most local level we seek to be known as reconcilers and peacemakers in our families and communities. That is what is to be reimagined: not being blocked by the possibilities that we see but inspired to hope by the possibilities God sees and that we hear in solitary and collective prayer and study of the Bible.

CROSSING DIVIDES

I wrote earlier about my friend in America who visited the other churches in his area, not just the ones that were like his own. I also wrote about Brother Andrew, crossing the boundaries of the Iron Curtain with bibles and bringing hope to Christians being persecuted, later crossing other boundaries to meet terrorist leaders. In both cases they reimagined the situation with hope injected into it and with contact and humanity as part of it.

Not all of us, or even many of us, will have such dramatic opportunities as Andrew. However, the beginning of crossing a boundary is to try and imagine what everything would look like if that boundary were not there. After that comes the hard work that is described in the rest of this book. The six plates of Part II need to be spun and kept spinning. We need the habits of curiosity and being present. We need to know and understand the barriers. Most of all we will want our reimagined vision to be seen, even in small ways, so that it is caught more and more widely.

Crossing divides cannot be about us. It is easy – I have often seen it and even more often been tempted by it – to want to be known as a peacemaker. The recognition looks wonderful from the outside. Yet when you meet the winners of Nobel Peace Prizes, often they see it as slightly embarrassing to have been treated as the hero. They also know the cost.

A few years ago, I met a doctor who works with the huge number of women in eastern Congo who have been raped during the war. Denis Mukwege treats them physically and psychologically. His faith and work are utterly inspiring. He does not seek attention for himself but for them. He took the Nobel Peace Prize for them and he takes the death threats made against his work for himself. That is the reality of someone who saw the condition of the women and reimagined what could happen to them. Before he received the prize, he was almost unknown. He crossed the boundary to those who were excluded from their communities, unvalued by their attackers and without hope, and brought all those blessings of value, inclusion and hope with him. He also knew that he had not acted alone. In his acceptance speech he spoke of those women who had served with him at immense risk, and paid tribute to the survivor of sexual violence in conflict, Nadia Murad, who was honoured equally with him, and is equally remarkable.

The question when facing a boundary, whether it is resistance to global action on climate change, or to new patterns of interracial relations, or to reuniting a community that has fallen out, is what reconciliation would look like. It will very seldom if ever be in our image. It will even less often look like overwhelming victory for one side and the complete destruction of the other – evil ideas may need to be destroyed, but not people.

The second question is to reimagine the steps by which things could change. What relationships could be different? How could there be a way of dealing with the particular causes of division that put justice front and centre and gave dignity to all involved?

The third question is to imagine who I would like to work with, and then to ensure that the imagination is disciplined by an intention of diversity. To cross boundaries well we need to be in relationship with people on both sides of the boundaries, so that the collective decision making has the benefit of good navigators on both sides. Perhaps it is worth beginning by asking what you are praying for, and who.

DISAGREEING WELL

'On some things we will never agree.' So spoke one friend in Liverpool about another who was and is a 'Blue', an Everton supporter, as opposed to a 'Red', a Liverpool supporter. And they don't. But they are friends. Those who come from Liverpool and are football supporters will understand that a friendship like that can be noticeable.

In their case it did not take a major effort of reconciliation. After all, they each married one of two sisters and are the closest of family as well.

Disagreeing well, in most circumstances, is very much more complicated. It may be over a fundamental point. I have several Muslim friends with whom I disagree on the most basic of issues: the very nature of God. Yet we are friends, we seek each other's company and enjoy it when we meet.

Even that, though, is not disagreeing well enough yet, because disagreeing well is tested by the circumstances of disagreeing over something very important, and doing so with passion, and yet maintaining a relationship. Within the Church of England and the Anglican Communion, among the many people I deeply admire and whose example inspires me are a whole group of bishops who form close relationships with others with whom they disagree profoundly and publicly. They meet annually, in 2020–21 on Zoom, of course. They focus their discussions on the questions of human sexuality, same-gender marriage and a host of related issues. It is a very practical approach to reconciliation within the Communion.

At the Anglican Consultative Council of 2018, in Hong Kong, there was a motion put forward about human sexuality. Different people spoke with powerful views and different approaches. It was heated and difficult. Among them were some of those who had met in the group I had just described. They did not minimize the differences, hide their passions or settle for fuzzy compromise. They did speak to each other afterwards, listen to each other well, be present with each other and continue to meet. That is disagreeing well. They recognized that the subject being discussed was of immense importance, so much so that feelings and tempers would be touched. It was also recognized that those who disagreed might be wrong but were not evil. They were part of the family.

Practising Forgiveness

If disagreeing well is a steep hill, then forgiveness can be a vertical cliff face. The number of global and irreconcilable or deeply intransigent conflicts there are is a major subject of academic discussion on peacebuilding. We probably know of or experience relationships where forgiveness seems beyond reach under any circumstances. Many people simply cannot forgive themselves.

Forgiveness is not achieved by grovelling when one does not believe one has done wrong. It is often a way out of an argument. Metaphorically, you cross your fingers while saying sorry, in your mind feeling that you are right. All that does is store up a sense of bitter self-righteousness that will explode even more damagingly in the end. The same thing can happen at a national as well as an individual level. Feeling forced to admit blame in which one does not believe was behind much of the deep resentment in Germany after the Treaty of Versailles in 1919. It leads to a desire for revenge, in the individual as well as the community.

There are many other ways, but they require reimagining as well as the other habits. It is necessary to ask oneself, and often others, what forgiveness would look like. An objective but loving and accepting view will help see one's own responsibilities. The TRC in South Africa led many participants to a proper sense of their own participation in evil deeds and the need for them to accept fault and seek forgiveness. Conversely, hearing and seeing such transformation permitted forgiveness in some of the most unlikely of cases.

Reimagining forgiveness is a hard task as either perpetrator or victim. It is so easy to make it a duty that abuses the already abused. Survivors of abuse often rightly push back vehemently against cheap views of forgiveness or the immense pain that forgiveness will often cause to the forgiver.[3] There are many ways of getting to the place of forgiveness far more slowly and circuitously in which the victim begins to see themselves in a new light and to sense that their power to forgive or withhold forgiveness is very great and in some cases puts the perpetrator within their hands. As has already been said, there is a big difference between forgiveness and forgetting the consequences. The statement 'I forgive you, but you must still carry your punishment from the law' is perfectly coherent. It recognizes that crimes and oppression are communal and not purely individual, even the dreadful ones of abuse and discrimination, even the most terrible crime of murder.

Reimagining forgiveness begins within oneself, in complete honesty with God and complete openness to learning to know that one is loved. That is a first step of many, but a strong one.

Risking Hope

Horses are not my favourite thing. They are lovely to see, some of the most beautiful animals, and I deeply admire good riding. Purely personally, however, I notice that they have teeth at the front and powerful hind legs and hooves at the back. They are intelligent enough to know what they want and big enough to choose it. As a child, when I fell off a horse, rather than getting back on I decided to go sailing in small, tippy dinghies. No teeth, no hooves, no brain. Less fear.

Getting back on is very difficult even in something as unimportant as a riding lesson. Getting back on is a wholly more difficult thing when you have fallen away from hope and risked everything in hope of reconciliation.

For exactly this reason most reconciliation work, or even mediation work within it, is better done in pairs or teams than by oneself. Recent work in South Sudan has involved remarkable teams from numerous agencies. There have been no solitary stars. Reimagining hope is a joint exercise. It is also a systematic one.

It starts with acknowledging the problem and the failures. It does not use euphemisms like 'challenge' or 'opportunity', as in 'there is no such thing as a problem, there are only opportunities', to which one of my work colleagues replied to our mutual boss: 'in that case we are facing an insurmountable opportunity'. Honesty starts with finding reality because hope grows out of reimagining starting with where you are, not where you would like to be.

It continues with a reminder about the end vision. What is it you are trying to achieve? If it is for the COP conferences on climate change it might be world net-zero carbon emission by 2050 on a basis of just sharing of costs and benefits. There may be setbacks very early on but there will still be many other ways of getting there. The failed Copenhagen COP[4] of 2009 was followed eventually by the success of Paris in 2015. Holding the end vision in sight enables one to see the whole countryside and not just the immediate roadblock.

It may be that in a family dispute the end vision needs rethinking. Perhaps, rather than putting the marriage back together, it may be parting well and with care for all those affected.

It involves essentially a great deal of trying of ideas, of thinking, and starting with what should be rather than with the resources. Imagine first, then look for the resources to get there, and only if that fails imagine again on a different basis.

Risking hope requires the highest level of reimagination because reimagination's greatest enemy is despair. In the most intransigent disputes, hope is formed by coming back to my friend Bishop Désiré's adage: 'Do what you can, what God resources you to do, and leave the rest to God.' In that way, bit by bit the reimagining will rekindle the hope.

SUMMARY

- Reimagining is hard and seldom purely solitary.
- It is perspiration and detailed work as much as it is inspiration.
- It is a foundation for vision, which in turn feeds new and stronger vision.
- It is a habit, not an event. Every setback is met by it.

POINTS TO PONDER

- Are you imaginative? Who do you know who is? How does it happen?
- Looking at disputes of which you are aware, try the exercise of seeing afresh what the vision for success looks like and work backwards towards the reimagining needed to get there.
- If you are in despair, or caught by bitterness because of suffering, do not surrender; imagine who can help you and seek support.

13

Three Examples for Reflection

In this chapter we are going to look at three cases, at a very high level, but seeking to apply some of the lessons of this book to potential avenues for exploration. I am aware that in none of the three is there detailed discussion, and they are not included to give answers but to suggest humbly some examples of the very beginnings of application of some of the ideas of this book. I am equally aware of the huge complexity of the issues, and that vast numbers of people do nothing but work on them. I am not for a moment feeling that I know better!

There are two conflicts that are both universal and local. The first is climate change and the second is racism and ethnicity. Within the western democracies there is a third: the issue of populism (used here in the sense of manipulating genuine fears and grievances for the end of political power, not in order to find their solution. Of course, the issues are very often, even usually, genuine and need dealing with in genuine partnership and giving power to those who endure them.).

This last challenge of disagreeing well also exists in all other countries, including Russia, India, Pakistan, much of the Middle East and in many countries in Africa. However, the social situations underlying these countries are so radically different that they are not possible to consider here except in widely generalized form.

Climate Change: Human Conflict with the Planet

In the case of climate change the research is very well developed. The vast majority of scientists agree, and the objective evidence supports, the idea that the climate is changing and biodiversity is threatened, to a degree that will threaten the future habitability of large parts of the earth, especially in low-lying areas and in the Tropics.

It is also very widely agreed that these enormous changes are to a large extent human driven. There have been very many extreme changes before, but never at this speed and never with such a clear and unprecedented externality, human economic development, and its consequences in the emission of pollutants and carbon or other gases linked to global warming.

Since 2016, it is also widely agreed that the target for the twenty-first century should be to limit global warming to 1.5 °C above pre-industrial levels. The present outputs from human activity seem more likely to result in more than 2 °C – perhaps 2–3 °C, or even higher.

The mapping of the conflict is less clear, but some key features are easily seen.

- As discussed earlier, it is possible to see two major sides: the creation and the human race. However, that is a terrible over-simplification.

○ Human beings range from massive contributors per head both to a loss of biodiversity and to global warming, to those whose contribution is insignificant. In general the former are from relatively rich countries and the latter from the poorest, including people groups who are essentially non-contributors and thus are victims of the changes.

○ At the same time there is uncertainty about the impact on the climate in specific areas. Some places may become easier to inhabit and do relatively well. For example, the UK and especially its northern parts may become more open to new forms of agriculture where it is currently not warm enough. Whether this is true or not, the overall effect is likely to cause people movements of extraordinary size, the political impact of which will only be manageable with huge sacrifice or immense inhumanity.

○ 'Spoilers' are also identifiable by many. They are not a single block. Some disagree with the majority of scientists. Some agree but feel that morally it is not right to limit economic growth now for the sake of those yet unborn and that the discounted cost of future climate warming is less than the current cost of its prevention. Some have a vested interest in the economic rents and returns from economic activity that drives climate change. This includes companies, political parties, nations and individuals. They are in different moral as well as political categories. The first group

may widely be seen to be mistaken but it helps
no one to categorize them as wicked. Spoiler
is thus a bad term. The other groups have a
more dubious role. Finally, there are significant
shadow influences, especially in international
politics and in politics in the democracies.

- Risk capacities range vastly, and a RAM (Risk
Allocation Matrix; see Chapter 7) would be a
book in itself. Essentially, though, the strongest
players in the short term are human beings in
geographical areas that are less likely to be heavily
and adversely affected, and that also happen to
be, in some but by no means all cases, the richest.
In the short term the poorest in any country
are the most at risk, and the poorest countries
have the highest risks. In the long term, human
beings are likely to be the weaker party, and the
creation the dominant force, in the absence of
something extraordinary turning up in scientific
and technological aspects of climate control.

However, the adequacy of work breaks down when it
comes to relating.

- There is no universally trusted group to act
as a convenor and facilitator among the 197
states and far more people groups, lobbies
and interests.
- The human side is bitterly divided, at odds
with each other to the point of war on other
interests, and divergent in capacity. The creation
side is impersonal, a thing that is not open to
negotiation or discussion. It simply responds

to inputs in a way that we do not understand
adequately. It could be argued that the conflict
is within the human side, but that ignores the
consequences of failing to act.

- The sense of responsibility for creation has been
diluted by millennia of activity that did no
permanent harm, by religious teaching of various
traditions, and the huge extent of groups having
an impact so that everyone feels the problem is
someone else's.
- The mere fact of a common need does not seem
to break down the individual wills of nations
and groups.

The common good is thus not recognized and needs
establishing. At the same time the danger threatening
the planet should give a great incentive to every human
being, provided they have hope of some progress in their
lives and of adequacy of food, shelter and security.

The relating is therefore going to have to work hand
in glove with the relieving, and reconciliation to reduce
conflict and increase security must be a priority in
order to enable longer-term thinking and minimize
the possibilities of wars that prevent any further action
on climate.

For all human beings, the imminent threat of death
or the destruction of society will outweigh all longer-
term issues.

The urgent need is therefore to relieve need.

- The restarting of trade that is fair and open
will give huge incentives to innovation and will
reduce extreme poverty very rapidly indeed,

as has been seen in the last fifty years. The World Trade Organization is therefore a central structure for the necessary developments that will open the doors to better work on climate and biodiversity.

- In some places, this can only be done with aid offered at the UN's recommended 0.7 per cent level of Gross National Income. The giving of such aid to parts of the economy where the economic return is too long term for thinly capitalized and poor countries, such as infrastructure, health and above all, education, will ease the pressure towards a world climate change agreement sufficient to limit the temperature rise. Aid needs reimagining and political leadership must enable the richer parts of the world to be curious and present to see the impacts.

- Peacebuilding needs to be of the highest priority and enabled by every nation with good armed forces and the skills to enable local populations to be reconciled. Key areas to tackle must be, first, the arms trade, which must halt the flow of weapons and ammunition to conflicts. Second, anti-corruption and tax evasion is indispensable, and tax havens and lack of transparency must be ended. The largest financial centres, in particular London, the EU, Europe other than the EU, Singapore and the USA, together with those areas of dependency, can tackle this question. Legislation on an international basis needs to make tax evasion and money laundering even harder than now.

- The UN must have the capacity to stop conflicts, intervening early. This would need more cooperation from the permanent five members of the Security Council, the strengthening of regional and multilateral partners such as the African Union, and the embedding of mediation and reconciliation hubs in national and international security structures.
- But relieving must also be done at the most local level. Basic improvements are indispensable in green spaces within communities, in recycling even at household level, with incentives to alter behaviour. Added to that must be a huge effort in education. Excellent local practice will deepen the commitment to excellent national practice (middle out) and thus in its turn to global progress.

The risks involved are huge.

- The very large political risks of the sacrifices necessary by the currently rich to enable the poor to grow sufficiently to take their own steps against climate change are risks of a monumental nature. The major problem is pain now in exchange for survival and flourishing in fifty years. Those risks can only be decided by people voting, but must be encouraged by politicians and others leading. One essential is for the weight of sacrifice in each economy to be borne by the wealthy in the same way as globally it must be borne by the wealthiest economies.

- The role of faith groups, which account for over 80 per cent of humanity, is essential. Their leaders must take risks: of being responsible for teaching on the sacred relationship with creation, of meeting and leading, of taking responsibility for the errors of those who claim to follow their faith. Christians have to be the global foot-washers, by their service and example enabling others to be liberated to serve well. For church leaders, this will often mean the risk of laying aside prestige, partition and inter-church quarrels for the sake of God's call to be stewards of creation and lovers of the poor and suffering.
- One way of mitigating the pain of the sacrifice is through green technology, fiscally encouraged. Expertise cannot be allowed to be monopolized by one country. What benefits only a small group will never motivate the vast majority. If the vast majority is not motivated, the future is lost.
- The struggle to combat climate change is going to be one full of setbacks, with the outcome visible only after more than a century. Maintaining the impetus will be a great risk. Finding milestones that can be celebrated is a huge challenge.
- The risk of meetings failing, and of major economies taking a short-term advantage, and the risks of terrible diversions such as wars, make the need to cooperate in this area on which all should be able to share a vision a potential huge mitigator of risk in other areas of competition.

Reconciling, with all these challenges, offers great hopes and great difficulties.

- It will bring hope to see nations agree on objectives. The relationships built may enable other dangerous areas, such as nuclear weapons proliferation and use, to be addressed with greater mutual confidence.
- The endless meetings and necessary campaigns are a long road without much beautiful scenery or interesting diversions. What progress can be made to encourage resolution and resilience?
- Reconciliation must be at the three levels: top down, middle out and bottom up. On such a scale of issue as this, the top is the global, the middle the national/regional and the bottom the local. To reimagine at each level, to make the struggle present at all levels, to encourage presence and participation without elitism, all these habits will be necessary.

Resourcing is where it hurts.

- The sharing of costs is the largest problem of the day. Sacrifice, suffering and altruism are required.
- Resourcing must include the development of adequate scientific, mathematical, technological and cultural skills to enable civilizations to develop and grow in a way that is committed to the common good. This can only be done at a national level; any form of international paternalistic or imperialist top-down approach is utterly wrong. Yet it must be resourced to

give every person in any economy opportunity
to aspire, to compete, to be ambitious and yet
to serve.

In all these areas we have the skills. There is a need for a
trusted, diverse, transparent and effective global secretariat
to coordinate and advocate. The UN is made for such
things. There is also a need for brave leadership. That we
must see in the years up to 2030.

RACIAL AND ETHNIC DIFFERENCES
AND DIVISIONS

Racism and ethnic divisions are invariably born out of a
common fiction, which is summed up for the British in
a satirical poem by Daniel Defoe, who wrote *The True-
born Englishman* in 1701, when Britain had a Dutch king,
sandwiched between previous French, Welsh and Scottish
dynasties and our present German line:[1]

> Thus from a mixture of all kinds began
> That het'rogeneous thing, an Englishman:
> In eager rapes and furious lust begot
> Betwixt a painted Briton and a Scot ...
> In whose hot veins new mixtures quickly ran,
> Infus'd betwixt a Saxon and a Dane ...
> Fate jumbled them together, God knows how;
> Whate'er they *were* they're true-born English *now* ...
> A true-born Englishman's a contradiction,
> In speech an irony, in fact a fiction ...
> Since scarce one family is left alive
> Which does not from some *foreigner* derive.

Or to put it more bluntly, Professor Mary Mwiandi, former chair of the University of Nairobi's History department, said at a 2009 historians conference, 'We're all immigrants and we're all here.'[2] The loss of that reality is fertile ground for racism across the world.

In the case of climate change the biggest weakness is in the R of relating. In the case of race and ethnicity, including the challenges and suffering behind BLM, the areas of failure are much wider.

Researching is prolific but not agreed.

- In terms of the habits of reconciliation in the *Difference Course*, the effective segregation in many parts of many countries reveals the absence of curiosity, betrays the failure of presence and prevents reimagining.
- By failing to see the distinctions, there is radical over-simplification of failures that are different in different societies. The problems in race relations in the USA are very different from those in the UK or in France, to take three examples. For example, the UK has not since the end of serfdom had *legal* slavery in the way that many states in the USA did until the mid-nineteenth century. However, the prosperity of many English cities, especially Bristol, Gloucester and Liverpool, but indeed of the whole of what is now the UK, was built on the slave trade. In addition, the entire UK economy gained hugely from not only trading in slaves but also the related trades in the Golden Triangle of shipping goods to West Africa, slaves across the Atlantic, and sugar and other goods to

British ports. It is also worth remembering that the legacy of slavery in the UK is so profound that the compensation for the abolition of slavery in the British Empire only stopped being paid to the descendants of former slave owners in 2015.

- The British position is enormously complicated by the legacy of Empire, which has led to great diversity of religious and ethnic backgrounds since 1945. The simplification of all these factors into one category of BAME, when there is immense diversity within that grouping, also provides for lack of clear thinking and a recognition of proper responsibility by some among the White majority. As was discussed much earlier, many White people in the richest parts of the world are themselves deeply excluded from the benefits of economic growth and do not experience privilege in any meaningful sense.

- Another example is France, where the history of empire is very different and thus the minority ethnic groups tend to have a much higher proportion from North Africa. In the case of Black people in the UK, a high proportion of those who came from the Caribbean, and were and are so ill-treated, are of Christian and not Muslim tradition. Those of a Muslim background often come with the legacy of the British Empire more than that of slavery.

- There has also been a tendency for debate to become focused on highly controversial areas such as Critical Race Theory, as though

disproving it would somehow show there is
no problem with racism. Such self-unaware
approaches to the genuine issues of racism reveal
a lack of willingness to be present, to be curious
and to reimagine.

Thus, researching has done much, more than in almost
any other area of dispute and conflict, but has not resulted
in an acceptance of a basis of truth that reflects perception
and real experiences.

Relating has been alluded to in discussion of the issues
of the 'two hours of segregation' on a Sunday in the USA,
and in equivalent separated living in many other places,
including parts of UK cities, schools, housing and so
on. In France the suburbs of places like Paris reflect this
problem very significantly.

- Relating starts at the local. It must be the
  responsibility and vision of local groups, of
  intermediate institutions, to work hard with
  programmes like *Difference* and then seek in every
  possible way to encourage local gathering. Where
  this happens the results are superb, as can be seen
  by schemes in England like Near Neighbours.[3]
- Once again education must play a large role. Key
  issues to be addressed at local and regional levels
  must be differentials of health and education
  outcomes, standards of housing, language
  proficiency, and opportunities for high-quality
  higher and further education.
- There are increasingly good role models where
  relating is demonstrated. In many countries these
  are seen specially in sport. That is true in the UK.

- Challenges around public health and housing give a very good opportunity for building relationships within local government areas. So do local politics.
- One of the biggest challenges is the quality of relationships and not just the quantity. Do they permit the raising of genuine areas of concern and differences of perception? This is where the habits matter of being curious, being present and reimagining.
- A genuine area of controversy is free speech. The danger of facing the issues of racist behaviour is that fear of experiencing racism again, or of being called racist, lead to self-censorship. In that sense people are not present to each other and dare not be curious. The reality of the problem is handled in the USA by the First Amendment rights, and in other countries by tight restrictions. They represent two ends of a range. Truth is something that needs to see the lie in order to challenge it. Better to hear racist language and answer than to be unaware of lurking thoughts is an approach that has much to commend it. All that being said, encouragement to violence is always wrong.
- At the heart of relating, to quote a friend from an African British background, is that the issue of 'Whiteness' is a cultural disorder in everything we do. In other words, the whole way of living assumes being White (or, for that matter, male). I have heard this comment from many people who never speak of Critical Race Theory. The point being made, from a strongly

Christian and biblical view, is that change requires a shift in power, and a clearer sense of truth. In the conversation there was a very interesting metaphor, which I am still thinking about, involving Old Power in our society and New Power. Old Power is institutional; you have to fit. New Power is participative; you have to join in. Old Power is *Tetris*, New Power is *Minecraft*. Both forms of power are needed, but both need each other in order to balance the other's weakness.

Relieving need is a huge issue and very weakly addressed.

- The largest challenge is that of reparations. The historic legacy of slavery, Empire and racist attitudes linked to both has in many ways led to systemic discrimination. The question about reparations will have to be faced, and an answer found that is a sufficient sign and symbol of genuine relief of the needs caused by past actions. It cannot be right to say that the policies of past generations are not our fault, and thus should not be the subject of reparations, while on the other hand enjoying the results and fruits of those policies in terms of global power, of privilege, and of position internally and externally to our country, whichever it may be.
- The danger is that reparations will be so difficult to agree that at a national or international level the search for the right answer will take so

long that it will lead to no answer for several generations. Once again, the local matters. For example, Virginia Theological Seminary has a programme of tracing and seeking to support those who are the descendants either of those enslaved at the Seminary or of those who were employed there in the time of the Jim Crow laws. That can be done in many places.

· A clear area of reparations will be in working with countries that were affected by the slave trade to improve education and opportunity.

The issues of risking and reconciling will vary from country to country. There will never be a universal settlement, even in one society, because it is rightly impossible to work out who represents whom. Reconciliation in all these areas will be sociological, long term, local, and above all will require sacrifice by those who are in power. Each discrete area of discrimination will need looking at to ensure justice and truth. In some cases, this will be by a panel. The scandals of Windrush and associated racist actions come to mind. In other areas the key question will be representation in leadership. It is very noticeable that in the UK the Home Secretary in August 2021, the Chancellor of the Exchequer, the Business Secretary, the Health Secretary and the Cabinet minister who was president of COP 26 in Glasgow were all from a minority ethnic heritage. That would have been impossible even thirty years ago. Progress can be made, but it requires a continued determined effort, a vision and a fixed aim to see greater justice for all human beings, for all are made in the image of God.

HATRED AS THE GREAT GOOD

The third and last of these reflections is on the divisions
we find among ourselves, sometimes called populist, or
nationalist, but realistically each label misleads to some
degree. These divisions are as old as human beings for
they are founded on desires for power and desires to retain
power. Those who stir up these hatreds seek to enable
people to find their identity by finding their enemies.

In 2 Samuel 15, King David's son Absalom, returned
from exile, carries out a textbook *coup d'état*. The first
step is to stir up latent discontent within the kingdom.
This he does by supporting those who felt excluded and
'thus Absalom stole the hearts of the people of Israel'.
It is a classic approach, which culminated in a swift
military strike that capitalized on the popular support
he had. The pattern is equally familiar in modern times.
Conversely, the pattern of Jesus Christ and of his Church
when it acts rightly is not to seek power but to serve. The
revolutionary nature of all that Jesus did and all that God
does today is found in this rejection of the classic means
of taking power.

The extreme opposite characterizes many populist
rulers and leaders today, whose ability to gain traction in
their campaigns arises from using existing divisions, not
only some magic in the way they campaign or speak, or
in their policies.

The impact of divisions unreconciled – that is to say,
without the capacity to disagree well – is to open a society
and large groups of people to manipulation. By contrast,
the justice and goodness of God, in the words of Mary
the mother of Jesus in Luke 2, is seen in equality, the
humbling of the proud, the satisfaction of the needs

of the poor. To put it infinitely less poetically than the *Magnificat*, God is present and shows us a reimagined world of justice, of forgiveness and of love. A church that does not identify with that vision but rather seeks its own power loses its soul.

In the UK, the USA and many countries in Europe and around the world, great changes have taken place, often through democratic votes that did demonstrate the voice of the people, such as the Brexit referendum vote in the UK, but leaving behind a deeply fractured and angry society. On 6 January 2021 a crowd stormed the Capitol Building in Washington DC, claiming that victory for their candidate in the US elections of November 2020 had been stolen. The claim of a rigged election is very often the cry of those who lose, but to see sights such as occurred on that day and to experience the bitter divisions that continue was deeply shocking to many with no personal interest in who was elected.

What can be done about this anger? Is such a thing as a reconciled society possible to imagine?

The strength of populist leaders is considerable as a result of political skills of a high order. In a way that mimics the *Difference Course*, but with motives of power rather than peacebuilding, they begin with listening, a habit of paying attention, being present to those whose voices are not normally heard. The contrast was often seen, and still is heard, among so-called elites, who openly, or behind closed doors, appear to be contemptuous of the voices of large groups of people.

Virtues such as patriotism are too often derided or ignored as old-fashioned and out of date. There is contempt for many who are genuinely concerned about the changing nature of the country, whether through social change, immigration, economic impact, the financial engineering of international capital in the City of London, Wall Street and a thousand other centres, and above all the sense that they exist to be the objects of other people's manipulation. In the words of the UK Brexit campaign, people want to take back control.

What is seen above all is an absence of research and relationship. To put it simply, many of those with money and power don't know what the struggle is for those without it and don't care. Whether genuinely or not – it is too easy to judge over hastily on that question – many populist leaders, for want of a better description, do 'get it'. Or, at the very least, they sound as if they do. They channel the anger that is felt in communities that for generations lived in one way and that, through no fault of their own, have seen their ways of life changed. In the north-east of England in the 1960s there were more than eighty thousand people employed in the mines. Today there are none. In Liverpool, at the same time, up to forty thousand people worked in the docks and related industries; today it is less than one-tenth of that figure.

Anger and discontent are reasonable and proper reactions from people who find their world changing and whose leaders do not appear to be paying attention. To combine rapid economic change with rapid social change only adds to that sense of insecurity as communities feel disrupted.

The relieving of need, in the absence of a genuine understanding of those needs, does not make a difference, even if done with the best of intentions. To use the language of the habits encouraged in the *Difference Course*, being curious leads to understanding, being present to relationship, and those two enable a reimagining.

The risks in such divisions are on one side from those who seek to use disrupted economic and social conditions to gain power, and who point to perceived and often real injustices. On the other side, the risks are accentuated by distanced and mechanical systems of care and mutual support. The impersonality of government actions is a direct result of the fact that they are not mediated through the local. Archbishop William Temple pointed to the essential nature of intermediate institutions, those that exist between the state and the household, that are sometimes voluntary and in other cases small businesses, social clubs, churches, schools, hospitals and an infinite number of others. Those in them know their areas, recognize needs and are capable of meeting them.

The infrastructure for meeting needs exists, through everything from parliamentary, political constituency associations in the UK to local mayors in France and to very strong faith communities and other local charitable groups in the USA. Local governments, when properly funded, are accustomed to meeting needs.

One of the earliest and most crucial developments in epidemiology took place in the Soho area of London in 1854. A severe outbreak of cholera was in full swing. The local curate, the Revd Henry Whitehead, working under the leadership of Dr John Snow, and with support from Florence Nightingale, mapped and identified the source of the infection as one water pump. Although removing that pump helped, the more significant change was in the understanding of the causes of cholera as being waterborne, not airborne.

The point of what happened was that it was local, as public health is to this day. Local actions based in local knowledge and relationships are critical for the national or global changes required.

Reconciling divided societies is the ultimate test of whether we can find the will and determination to overcome issues of privilege and power and work simultaneously from the bottom up, middle out and top down.

Reconciling happens when there is a level of trust created by the previous Rs, when people see genuine curiosity based in love and care, when they experience relationships, when needs are met and when people take risks. To map the conflicts of our societies is too large a task, and the different local levels are too varied. Yet some things we can see, based around inequalities and injustices. Resourcing reconciliation requires a shift in the way government works in divided societies, from doing to changing to doing with.

As mentioned earlier in this book, one area of work going on is the /together campaign. That includes a vast range of groups of all sorts and opinions in the UK and is designed to demonstrate that there is much in common. It contains the potential for work at all levels. It is only one of numerous possibilities.

There is nothing inevitable about societies divided by hate. It is possible to disagree well. Yet, as in other areas, it requires the empowering of the local, not the distanced actions of an impersonal state. It is an economic process, but it is very far from being only that. It also requires moral imagination, deep relationships, profound risk taking, thoughtful research, adequate resourcing and long-term work. What it offers is not a society that has conquered all its problems, but one that has the structures and trust to face anything with resilience.

14

Conclusion

Reconciliation is a work of courage, not so much from the peacebuilder but supremely for those caught in conflict. The image of the Stalingrad Madonna is an image of the courage of God. God has chosen to be entrusted to a woman who is poor, helpless and in a country full of conflict. The living God is the lamb of the poem, fragile, vulnerable, dependent on someone who herself cannot keep them in safety. The setting of the Madonna is in the frozen terror of Stalingrad, the place of the consequence of the evils of power seeking and war. That is the most appropriate setting for the Lamb of God, who is the source of hope, life, liberty and light.

This is our true image of who God is. This is the reality that revolutionized us and the whole of creation. Our response to this 'light of the world' decides on what we are; in our response we judge ourselves, make our plea before God, and with our plea show by our choice of attitude to this fragility the evidence that our plea is true. The judgement of God is the perfect justice of giving us what we have chosen. To choose this helpless figure cradled in the arms of the helpless mother is to choose courage, the courage to receive love, hope, life: it is the courage to choose reconciliation with God and the journey of reconciliation with the world.

It does not matter whether it is the unknown sorrows of a life caught in a noxious relationship, or of workplaces surrounded by contempt and bullying, or the great decisions of life and death in global struggles. The will to peace is the will of courage, for it begins with seeing the humanity of the ones who hate us and whom we hate. Reconciliation offers the gift of overcoming ourselves, to listening attentively to others, seeking a reimagined humanity. Reconciliation develops our moral imagination in order to find other ways to disagree, ways of disagreeing well.

RECONCILIATION AS THE SOURCE OF HOPE

Imagine for a moment a world where the processes of politics were full of alternatives that included peacebuilding with our enemies. This is not a world where evil is easily overcome. Reconciliation requires the will to be exercised. The desire for power is so great in individuals and in nations that it will be taken by some at all costs.

The first point of conclusion is thus the least hopeful. There are some situations where reconciliation is not possible. Either one person involved is too proud, or too evil, or both. When we encounter genocide, the perpetrators must be stopped by any means necessary. We do not sit down to talk first, we seek a cessation of the carrying out of the evil. If it does not stop then action must be taken at once. The Rwandan Genocide could have been stopped very quickly. Even the Second World War could have been stopped by determined action in the mid-1930s. It is easy to judge in retrospect and hard to see clearly at the time. The moment a war starts, even in a righteous cause, all control of the future is lost. Yet sometimes it must happen.

The same is true at the most intimate level. Removing a parent where there is good reason to believe abuse is occurring in the home is drastic, irreversible and with a terrible long-term impact. Yet sometimes it must happen.

However, in most circumstances reconciliation is possible. This is where hope begins, provided we know what we are talking about.

First, a reminder of the definition: reconciliation is the transformation of destructive conflict into disagreeing well. The impact of disagreeing well may continue to be disagreement. It may be a state of well-contained hostility. It may mean the end of a marriage. But it will always open new possibilities of mitigating the harm, at the least, and of bringing genuine healing, at most.

Second, there is hope because reconciliation, over a lengthy period, offers the possibility of forgiveness, of the victim being liberated from the perpetrator's control, whether that is exercised through power or through the lingering hatred of the perpetrator. Either way, they remain a presence. Forgiveness is the most final form of revenge. It is often desperately hard. It cannot be used against a victim to blackmail them into waiving the right to justice. It is something else apart from justice, it is the chance of freedom and a future. In Christian understanding, in some extraordinary mystery of beauty and love, God on the cross brought together justice and mercy, opening not only the gift of forgiveness to all who accept it but their own forgiving of themselves, and even others.

Third, reconciliation is a way of hope because it requires the stronger party to make the sacrifice of choosing to live with the weaker and not to control, dominate and rule them. It is a sacrifice made by God out of the purest of love, love so pure that it sent a beam of light through the whole of creation: the light of Christ. It is also a sacrifice called for if the strong recognize their own need of reconciliation. Whether it is with the creation, with ethnic minorities, with those who are different, with the fragile and weak in a community, the sacrifice opens the way to build beautiful places in which to live. It is the way, at its best, to destroy enemies by making them friends, and at the worst to remove fear and anxiety from the places we live and the relationships we have.

Fourth, reconciliation opens the way to justice and truth. When sacrifice is made, then truth can be told. When truth is told, justice and mercy can meet and can be seen to be real. Justice before there is the beginning of reconciliation is almost always suspect, either because it is justice imposed by the strong or because the truth is not clear.

Pre-emptive Reconciliation a Necessity for All Our Futures

A world of power seeking and dominance by the strong depends for its future on the flimsiest of foundations. It depends on the consistent benevolence of the strong, caring for the weak. That only has to be said to be unbelievable.

At present there are approximately fifty significant conflicts in the world. At the same time, in many areas the circumstances of economics and challenges to historic sources of power are leading to talk of a second cold war. Some see the activities of cyber conflict as already a form of that war heating up. Nuclear proliferation remains a serious threat and the impetus towards disarmament has been lost. Climate change will accentuate the threats and dangers of the next fifty years.

It is easily forgotten that the world now possesses the capacity to kill every living thing, including every person. The nuclear strategies have no after-plan, for what happens once the buttons are pressed? The obvious answer is: 'Then we are all dead.' The idea that such an approach can be called a strategic move would be called insane if put forward by an individual, but is taken for granted when advanced by a government.

National and civil conflicts are taking place in the context of a world with an unprecedented capacity for destruction through nuclear, chemical, biological and cyber weapons and with an unprecedented threat caused by its normal economic activities and their impact on the creation. Conflict is always profoundly dangerous and usually deeply wrong. For it to happen amid such other dangers is beyond any degree of foolishness. Reconciliation is an essential.

In the face of all these threats, very often reconciliation will be impossible. So it is essential that there is pre-emptive reconciliation. Every nation should see reconciliation as a routine part of diplomacy, not a fire hose to put out an existing inferno. Pre-emptive reconciliation acts in a way that most will not notice. I remember a primary-school joke I heard as a child. A person stands by their gate. A neighbour asks, 'Why have you painted your gate pink?' 'It keeps the elephants away.' 'But there are no elephants round here!' 'You see, it works.'

Even if we are willing to spend scores of billions of dollars on armed forces, which we do, then some precautions make sense to reduce the extreme cost of their use. If we are willing to risk the future of the planet with nuclear arsenals, then working out how not to use them is obvious. Nations, communities, churches should all invest in developing pre-emptive reconciliation. It saves pain, time, money and, in the end, it saves life. The use at national level of mediation and peacebuilding units within every diplomatic service should be as routine as having a police force, or a health check-up.

Even in what we all hope is the more likely scenario – that the nations of the world learn to mitigate and contain conflict, that no nuclear outbreak happens, and that climate change is faced and dealt with – reconciliation is indispensable.

The capacity of human beings to disagree well has never been good, but the damage done by our failure to do so is vastly amplified by modern communications. On the day I write this, in mid-2021, there are reports of midwives having their lives threatened because they advocate vaccinations against COVID-19. The disagreement is tolerable, its form is evil.

In some places there are suggestions of near censorship to control forms of communication about the vaccines and the COVID-19 virus. A correction will always lead to censoring truth as well as lies.

Reconciliation offers the hope of vigorous and free differences of opinion without fear, of truth challenging lies without lies retaliating violently. It is the example of God. Even for the atheist it is the call of wisdom.

In this book the training suggested, the pattern set out and the needs described are a beginning. The *Difference*

Course has many alternatives, and it is my hope that further and more advanced training will follow quickly.

This book has tried to look at the reasons for reconciliation, to describe one – among many – patterns for it to happen, and to encourage the habits that make it possible. My prayer is that many will seek their own route to share in reconciliation, to start groups that will advocate and train others, and that will seek to make disagreeing well part of how we live at every level from household to global.

Acknowledgements

Too many people have been involved in this book to thank them all. To start with there are those who took part in seminars early in 2021 and while I was at Trinity College Cambridge, in the summer of 2021, where the research and first writing was done. Professor Anthony Reddie, The Very Reverend Dr Mandy Ford, Dr Gary Bell, The Baroness Reverend Maeve Sherlock OBE, Bill Marsh, The Reverend Canon Stephanie Speller, Alex Evans, Professor Miroslav Volf, Professor (or Father) Emmanuel Katongole, Pádraig Ó Tuama, Mariam Tadros Lord John Alderdice, General Sir Adrian Bradshaw KCB OBE, Roxaneh Bazergan, Irenée Herbert, Dame Karen Pierce, Professor Alasdair Coles, Professor Pumla Gobodo-Madikizela, Professor Simone Schnall, Professor Manos Tsakiris, Professor Miles Hewstone, Sofia Carozza (PhD student and Marshall Scholar Cambridge University), Revd Dr Tim Jenkins; Revd Catherine Matlock, Onjali Rauf, Canon Sarah Snyder, Dr Zaza Elsheikh, Dr Mukulika Banerjee, Dr Fenella Cannel, Dr Carlton Turner, Dr Ibram X. Kendi, Ebonee Davis (PhD student at Howard University), The Most Revd Michael B. Curry, Dr Catherine Meek, The Reverend Canon Cornelia Eaton, The Reverend Canon Stephanie

Spellers, Dr Kristopher Norris, The Revd Dr Katherine Grieb, Dr Nalini M. Nadkarni, The Reverend Canon Peter G. Kreitler, Martha C. Franks, The Reverend Gwynn Crichton, The Reverend Melanie Mullen, Dr Robert P. Jones, The Reverend Dr Molly F. James, The Reverend Gregory O. Brewer, The Right Reverend Martyn Minns, The Reverend Dr Canon C. K. Robertson, The Reverend Valerie Mayo, The Right Reverend Dr George Sumner, Amber D. Noel.

I am especially grateful to Professor Emeritus David Ford, for wise advice and wonderful encouragement over many years, and to his wife Deborah, similarly. Also to Dr Robert Heaney, whose book on post-colonial theology is so inspiring, and to the Reverend Professor Michael Banner and his wife Sally for yet more hospitality and for organizing the sabbatical term.

I thank Trinity College Cambridge, Master, Senior Tutor and others (especially the Fellows' Eight that kept me exercised) for their gracious and generous provision of space to study.

The first readers whose comments were invaluable were Katherine Richards, Joanna Alstott, Amelia Sutcliffe, Revd Dr Flora Winfield, Martha Jarvis, Kiera Phyo, Revd Dr Isabelle Hamley, Peter Welby, Chris Cox, Keziah Stephenson and Christopher Long.

Over the years I have learned from so many people. The reconciliation team at Lambeth Palace and Coventry Cathedral have taught me greatly, so I thank them especially.

The number of people I encountered who inspired me is huge. I owe especial thanks to Anglican archbishop Josiah Fearon and to Roman Catholic bishop Matthew Kukah. I add also Pastor James Wuye and Imam Ashafa (the Pastor and the Imam) in Kaduna, Archbishop Emmanuel Egbunu, Archbishop Benjamin Kwashi, Claudeline Mukanirwa and so many more that I cannot count them. Above all have been the huge numbers of women who have sought peace and pursued it, whose names, in the old expression from the First World War, are known only to God, but whose courage has transformed those around them.

My colleagues in the office have done a huge amount, especially David Porter, Emma Ineson, Tim Thornton. The hard work of organizing, sorting and making diaries work was through Joanna Alstott and Katherine Richards, as well as Amelia Sutcliffe.

I am very grateful to Robin Baird-Smith, a kind and thoughtful editor, and to Bloomsbury for patience, support and probing questions. Also to Nick Fawcett for his careful copyediting of the manuscript.

The cover is a production of the very remarkable artist, Timur d'Vatz.[1] His pictures are influenced by iconography and medieval art. I find them profoundly moving and his creation of such depth of art on the cover is a treasure.

And, of course, most of all, the family! In every way they educate, train and support, especially Caroline, my wife, whose own ministry of reconciliation with women leaders is so inspiring.

Reading List

In addition to works referred to in the Notes, you may find the
  following helpful:

Azevedo, R. T., S. N. Garfinkel, H. D. Critchley and M. Tsakiris,
  eds (2017), 'Cardiac afferent activity modulates the expression
  of racial stereotypes', *Nature Communications*, 8 (13854).
Baer, T. and S. Schnall (2021), 'Quantifying the cost of decision
  fatigue: suboptimal risk decisions in finance', *Royal Society
  Open Science*, 8 (201059).
Baez, S., E. Herrera, A. García, et al. (2017), 'Outcome-oriented
  moral evaluation in terrorists', *Nature Human Behaviour*, 1
  (0118).
Barton, M. (2005), *Rejection, Resistance and Resurrection:
  Speaking Out on Racism in the Church*, London: Darton,
  Longman & Todd Ltd.
Brendtro, L., M. Brokenleg and S. Van Bockern, eds
  (1990), *Reclaiming Youth at Risk: Our Hope for the Future*,
  Bloomington: National Educational Service.
Brett, Mark G. and J. Havea, eds (2014), *Colonial Contexts and
  Postcolonial Theologies: Story-Weaving in the Asian-Pacific*, New
  York: Palgrave Macmillan.
Bruneau, E. G. and R. Saxe (2012), 'The power of being
  heard: the benefits of "perspective-giving" in the context of
  intergroup conflict', *Journal of Experimental Social Psychology*,
  48 (4): 855–66.

Carlson, J. and A. Dumont, (1997), *Bridges in Spirituality: First Nations' Christian Women Tell their Stories*, Etobicoke: United Church Publishing House.

Carvalhaes, C., ed. (2015), *Liturgy in Postcolonial Perspectives: Only One Is Holy*, New York: Palgrave Macmillan.

Charleston, S. and E. Robinson, eds (2015), *Coming Full Circle: Constructing Native Christian Theology*, Minneapolis: Fortress Press.

Clarke, S. (2014), 'World Christianity and postcolonial mission: a path forward for the twenty-first century', *Theology Today*, 71 (2): 192–206.

Coates J. M. and J. Herbert (2008), 'Endogenous steroids and financial risk taking on a London trading floor', *Proceedings of the National Academy of Sciences of the United States of America*, 105 (16): 6167–72.

de Sousa Santos, B. (2018), *The End of the Cognitive Empire: The Coming of Age of Epistemologies of the South*, North Carolina: Duke University Press.

DeYoung, P. A. (2015), *Understanding and Treating Chronic Shame: A Relational/Neurobiological Approach*, London: Routledge.

Douglas, I. T. and K. Pui-lan, eds (2001), *Beyond Colonial Anglicanism: The Anglican Communion in the Twenty-First Century*. New York: Church Publishing.

Fanon, F. (1967), *Black Skin, White Masks*, New York: Grove Press.

Fanon, F. (1967), *Wretched of the Earth*, Harmondsworth: Penguin Books.

Gobodo-Madikizela, P. (2003), *A Human Being Died That Night: A South African Story of Forgiveness*. Boston: Houghton Mifflin.

Gobodo-Madikizela, P. (2015), 'Psychological repair: the intersubjective dialogue of remorse and forgiveness in the aftermath of gross human rights violations', *Journal of the American Psychoanalytic Association*, 63 (6): 1085–1123.

Haidt, J. (2012), *The Righteous Mind: Why Good People are Divided by Politics and Religion*, New York: Allen Lane.

Heaney, R. S. (2019), *Post-Colonial Theology: Finding God and Each Other Amidst the Hate*, Eugene: Cascade Books.

Horsley, R. (2002), *Jesus and Empire: The Kingdom of God and the New World Disorder*, Minneapolis: Fortress Press.

Jewett, R., ed. (2011), *The Shame Factor: How Shame Shapes Society*, Eugene: Cascade Books.

Joh, W. A. (2006), *Heart of the Cross: A Postcolonial Christology*, Louisville: Westminster John Knox Press.

Lederach, J. P. (1997), *Building Peace: Sustainable Reconciliation in Divided Societies*, Washington DC: United States Institute of Peace Press.

Lederach, J. P. (2010), *The Moral Imagination: The Art and Soul of Peacebuilding*, Oxford: Oxford University Press.

Lederach, J. P. (2014), *Reconcile: Conflict Transformation for Ordinary Christians*, Harrisonburg: Herald Press.

Malina, B. (2001), *The New Testament World: Insights from Cultural Anthropology*, Louisville: Westminster John Knox Press.

Marzouk, S. (2018), 'Famine, migration, and conflict: the way of peace – a reading of Genesis 26', in D. Schipani, et al. (eds), *Where Are We? Pastoral Environments & Care for Migrants: Intercultural & Interreligious Perspectives*, 3–18, Düsseldorf: Society for Intercultural Pastoral Care and Counselling.

Merz, J. (2020), 'The culture problem: how the honor/shame issue got the wrong end of the anthropological stick', *Missiology: An International Review*, 48 (2): 127–41.

Milevska, S., ed. (2016), *On Productive Shame, Reconciliation and Agency*, Berlin: Sternberg Press.

Nash, S. (2020), *Shame and the Church: Exploring and Transforming Practice*, London: SCM Press.

Neyrey, J. (1998), *Honor and Shame in the Gospel of Matthew*, Louisville: Westminster John Knox Press.

Owen, D. (2011), *In Sickness and Power*, London: Methuen Publishing Ltd.

Pattison, S. (2000), *Shame: Theory, Therapy, Theology*, Cambridge: Cambridge University Press.

Pettigrove, G. and N. Parsons (2012), 'Shame: a case study of collective emotion', *Social Theory and Practice*, 38 (3): 504–30.

Reardon, S. (2018) 'Columbia: after violence', *Nature*, 557 (7703): 19–24.

Reddie, A. (2019), *Theologising Brexit*, London: Routledge.

Reddie, A. and M. Jagessar (2007), *Postcolonial Black British Theology: New Textures and Themes*, London: Epworth Press.

Rossall, J. (2020), *Forbidden Fruit and Fig Leaves: Reading the Bible with the Shamed*, London: SCM Press.

Rowe, N. and S. Marzouk (2014), 'Christian disciplines as ways of instilling God's shalom for postcolonial communities: two reflections', in K. H. Smith, J. Lalitha and L. D. Hawk (eds), *Evangelical Postcolonial Conversations: Global Awakenings in Theology and Praxis*, 224–41, Downers Grove: InterVarsity Press.

Schnall, S., J. Haidt, G. L. Clore and A. H. Jordan (2008), 'Disgust as embodied moral judgment', *Personality and Social Psychology Bulletin*, 34: 1096–1109.

Schnall, S., K. Harber, J. Stefanucci and D. R. Proffitt (2008), 'Social support and the perception of geographical slant', *Journal of Experimental Social Psychology*, 44: 1246–55.

Smith, K. H., J. Lalitha and D. D. Hawk, eds (2014), *Evangelical Postcolonial Conversations: Global Awakenings in Theology and Praxis*, Downers Grove: InterVarsity Press.

Strathern, M. (2000), *Audit Cultures*, London: Routledge.

Sugirtharajah, R. S. (2001), *The Bible and the Third World: Precolonial, Colonial, and Postcolonial Encounters*, Cambridge: Cambridge University Press.

Sugirtharajah, R. S. (2002), *Postcolonial Criticism and Biblical Interpretation*, Oxford: Oxford University Press.

Swinton, J. (2007), *Raging with Compassion*, Grand Rapids: William B. Eerdmans Publishing Co.

Swinton, J. (2012), *Dementia: Living in the Memories of God*, Grand Rapids: William B. Eerdmans Publishing Co.

Swinton, J. (2018), *Becoming Friends of Time*, Waco: Baylor University Press.

Tajfel, H. (1970), 'Experiments in intergroup discrimination', *Scientific American*, 223 (5): 96–103.

Tsakiris, M. (2020), 'Politics is Visceral', *Aeon*, 18 September. Available online: https://aeon.co/essays/politics-is-in-peril-if -it-ignores-how-humans-regulate-the-body (accessed on 21 June 2021).

Turner, C. (2020), 'Could you be loved? BAME presence and the witness of diversity and inclusion', in C. Ross and H. Southern (eds), *Bearing Witness in Hope: Christian Engagement in Challenging Times*, London: SCM Press.

Turner, C. (2020), *Overcoming Self-Negation*, Eugene: Pickwick Publications.

van der Kolk, B. A. (2014), *The Body Keeps the Score: Brain, Mind, and Body in the Healing of Trauma*, New York: Viking.

Volf, M. (1996), *Exclusion and Embrace: An Exploration of Identity, Otherness, and Reconciliation*, Nashville: Abingdon Press.

Notes

INTRODUCTION

1 Part of the last poem (*Agnus Dei*) in a six-part 'agnostic Mass' entitled 'Mass for the Day of St Thomas Didymus' by Denise Levertov, *Candles in Babylon*, 113–15; also in *The Collected Poems of Denise Levertov*, 677–8. Found in David Ford's Theological Commentary on John's Gospel.

2 See *Enemy at the Gates* from 2001 for an example of a powerful film. *Stalingrad* by Antony Beevor (1998) is a superb history of the battle, traumatic to read.

3 For those who do not know the story there are many sources, starting with www.coventrycathedral.org.uk, The medieval cathedral and parish church was destroyed in a great bombing raid on 14 November 1940. The Provost of Coventry, Richard Howard, established it as a centre of reconciliation from the end of the Second World War, symbolized by a cross of nails that fell from the burning timbers to the floor of the cathedral. A new cathedral was completed in 1962, at right angles to the old, and linked by a great window so that the two go together as a symbol of death and resurrection. The Community of the Cross of Nails is a worldwide association of over two hundred centres that have crosses of nails or a non-Christian symbol, which work at reconciliation in their own contexts.

4   David F. Ford, *A Theological Commentary on the Gospel of John*, Baker Academic, a division of Baker Publishing Group, Grand Rapids, MI, 2021, (hereafter Ford, *John*).
5   Difference.rln.global.

CHAPTER 1

1   https://www.gov.uk/government/publications/global -britain-in-a-competitive-age-the-integrated-review-of -security-defence-development-and-foreign-policy.
2   Attributed to many people, including President Abraham Lincoln, Mark Twain and Dr Martin Luther King.
3   *On War*, Princeton University Press (date unknown), p. 87.
4   For developed discussion see Rowan Williams, *On Augustine*, Bloomsbury, 2016, Chapter 12, 'Augustinian Love', especially page 192. (Hereafter RW.)
5   RW, p. 185.
6   RW, p. 149, footnote 11.
7   RW, p. 55.
8   *Critical Race Theory: The Key Writings that Shaped the Movement*, ed. Crenshaw et al., The New Press, 1995, pp. 276–90.
9   Discussion with Revd Canon Dr Isabelle Hamley was very valuable here. She quotes Luce Irigaray as saying that Descartes seeks to 'give birth to himself', an act of 'astonishingly arrogant solipsism'.
10 Seen as a signifier of PTSD in the *Diagnostic and Statistical Manual of Mental Disorders*.
11 A powerful examination of the nature of monastic identity and its relationship to the world and cultures around it is found in Rowan Williams, *The Way of St Benedict*, Bloomsbury, 2020.
12 More details on the Archbishop of Canterbury's website.
13 See discussion on Ricoeur's Oneself as Another by Henry Venema in *Literature and Theology*, Vol. 16, No. 4, December 2002, around page 418.
14 Review of David Ford's *Self and Salvation* by John R. Sachs in *Theological Studies*, Vol. 6, No. 1, Washington, March 2001.

15 Williams, op. cit., especially Chapter 7, pp. 106ff.
16 Ford, *John*, pp. 416ff..

CHAPTER 2

1 *The Political Dimension of Reconciliation*, Ralf K.
Wüstenberg, Eerdmans, 2009, especially Part III,
pp. 197ff.
2 Revd Lucie Lunn, private paper quoting DeYoung (2015).
*Understanding and Treating Chronic Shame: A Relational/
Neurobiological Approach*, New York: Routledge. The next
paragraphs arise out of a personal conversation, 7 June
2021.
3 Using language to create a sense of low self-worth and/or
deep personal insecurity about anything from one's abilities
to one's sanity.
4 Conrad, 'Nostromo', commented on in 'Conrad and
Masculinity', PhD thesis by Emma Fox, 1995, p. 56.
5 'I'll put a girdle round about the earth in forty minutes',
Act II, Scene I.

CHAPTER 3

1 *The Moral Imagination: The Art and Soul of Building
Peace*, Oxford University Press, 2005. Professor John Paul
Lederach is a key writer in peace building. It is superbly
written by one of the wisest and bravest of facilitators and
thinkers about peace.
2 Lederach, *Moral Imagination*, p. 29.
3 *Global Britain in a Competitive Age: The Integrated Review of
Security, Defence, Development and Foreign Policy* describes
the government's vision for the UK's role in the world over
the next decade and the action we will take to 2025.
4 Lederach, *Moral Imagination*, p. 165.
5 Neurosciences Roundtable, Cambridge, 4 June 2021; see
notes for further reading.
6 Internally Displaced People. Technically, a refugee has
crossed an international border while an IDP is still within

their own country. It tends for those who have fled to be a difference without a distinction but has a major impact in international law, which governs the two categories differently giving more protection to refugees.

INTRODUCTION TO PART II

1 Hebrews 4.15.
2 Matthew 5.9 (NRSV).

CHAPTER 4

1 Op. cit.
2 One lawsuit on pollution concluded in the Dutch Courts as recently as January 2021, holding Shell liable, https://www.bbc.co.uk/news/world-africa-55853024.

CHAPTER 5

1 1 John 4.8.
2 Of course, nothing is ever exclusively the work of one person; Religions for Peace, Bill Vendley and many others were also central and only God knows who was the most important.
3 John 13.1 (NRSV).
4 Matthew, chapters 5–7, especially 7.1-5.
5 Because of a speech by Winston S. Churchill, 5 March 1946, in Fulton, Missouri: 'From Stettin in the Baltic to Trieste in the Adriatic an iron curtain has descended across Europe.'
6 His own account is in a book called *God's Smuggler*.
7 For a detailed examination see *The Political Dimension of Reconciliation*, Ralf K. Wüstenberg, trans. R. H. Lundell, Eerdmans, 2009.
8 Talal Asad, *On Suicide Bombing*, Columbia University Press, 2007, pp. 62–3.

CHAPTER 6

1 Identity carefully camouflaged, including nationality and denomination.
2 In John's Gospel, Jesus' key miracles are referred to as signs; in other words, actions that reveal the nature of Jesus and thus the nature of God.

CHAPTER 7

1 Luke 15.11-32 (NRSV).
2 Dr Isabelle Hamley, formerly Chaplain at Lambeth Palace, commented in a note: 'interesting to note that this is a very different approach to Western-centred models of justice and forgiveness, when we want offenders to make contrition (often multiple times) and victims to be able to go over their grievances repeatedly. The model here (as virtually everywhere in scripture) is of beginning with a willingness to embrace, from which other things follow.'
3 A diocese in England is a geographical area within which the churches are overseen by a bishop. The dean runs a cathedral, which is the main church of the diocese. The archbishop oversees a group of dioceses. A diocesan synod is a gathering of elected clergy and lay people led by the bishop to help decide on policy.
4 Sadly, it is yet to be invented.

CHAPTER 8

1 For example, *William Dalrymple*, 'The Anarchy', Bloomsbury, 2020 edition, p. 246.
2 *The Political Dimension of Reconciliation*, Ralf K. Wüstenberg, op. cit.
3 Glen Pettigrove and Nigel Parsons, *Social Theory and Practice*, Florida State University, Vol. 38, No. 3 (2012): 526; a very powerful and useful article.

4 Where the earliest Caribbean migrants to the UK were systematically deprived of their rights and even of their identities, being sent back to the Caribbean decades later.
5 *Financial Times*, 13 July 2021.
6 See *An Ethic for Christians and Other Aliens in a Strange Land*, William Stringfellow, Word Books, Waco, Texas, 1973.
7 Luke 5.1-11.

CHAPTER 9

1 Please see Chapter 2 and the Bibliography for further sources in this area.
2 Isaiah 2.4 (NRSV).
3 Ford 2021, op. cit., p. 297.
4 Appendix x, reproduced with permission.
5 *Christianity and Social Order*, 1942. For an updated approach, *Reimagining Britain*, Justin Welby, Bloomsbury, 2nd edition 2021.

CHAPTER 10

1 Found at difference.rln.global, +442078981016, hello@rln.global.
2 Prime Minister Neville Chamberlain used a phrase like this about Czechoslovakia in 1938.
3 Gordon Brown, *Seven Ways to Change the World*, Simon & Schuster, 2021.
4 Op. cit., p. 57.
5 Jonathan Sacks, *Morality: Restoring the Common Good in Divided Times*, Hodder, 2020.
6 *Essays on the French Revolution*, 1793.
7 *Difference: Your Guide*, 2020, p. 14.
8 Difference.rln.global.

CHAPTER 12

1 Another example of reimagining is that of Dr Sara Schumacher at St Mellitus College.

2 For an attempt at this please see Justin Welby, *Reimagining Britain*, Bloomsbury, 2018.

3 See a very remarkable examination of this: Dr Stephen Cherry, *Healing Agony: Re-imagining Forgiveness*, Bloomsbury, 2012.

4 Conference of the Parties, on facing climate change.

CHAPTER 13

1 Quoted by Professor John Lonsdale in an unpublished paper of 2021. The paper is a profound and superb reflection on the pre-colonial ethnic influences in East Africa. John goes on to say: 'So I make a serious if impractical suggestion: that the Ministry of Education award an annual prize, perhaps to be called the *Karibuni*, "You are all welcome", prize, to the high school student who best illustrates the multiple origins of her or his ethnic group in the style of Daniel Defoe.' One might suggest the same for the UK.

2 Lonsdale, op. cit.

3 Government-financed and often church-/faith-group-led interaction of different communities at local levels, administered by the Church of England Church Urban Fund.

ACKNOWLEDGEMENTS

1 www.timurdvatzstudio.com.

Index